YOU ARE

SOUL

Transform Your Life Now

MARIAN MASSIE

The spiritual teachings mentioned in this text are those derived from the author's personal experience and do not represent the official positions of Eckankar or Buddhism. The intent of the author is only to offer information of a general nature to help you on your quest for spiritual, mental, emotional and physical growth. In the event you may use any of the information in this book for yourself, which is your constitutional right, the author and the publisher assume no responsibility for your actions.

Library of Congress Catalog Number in Data Applied For

ISBN No. 0-9633140-3-3

Book and Cover Design — Paula Chance, Atlanta GA
Editor — Phyllis Mueller, Atlanta GA
Author's Photo — Brian Dourtry, Atlanta GA
Publisher — Advanced Perceptions Inc.

I dedicate this book to all
as a gift of love!
May the blessings be!

Contents

CHAPTER ONE

Responsibility

Oooooo — That horrid word.
What dark emotions it can evoke,
Dank and musty,
the root rot of growth.
Seriousness,
Authorities impinging on our rights,
But wait,
Let's shed more light…
A greater depth of understanding,
of this responsibility.
See it growing and happy.
Strong with joy and direction.
The master of its own evolution!
Ah, what a beautiful emotion it
evokes,
What beautiful life
it can create!

RESPONSIBILITY

All around the planet we continue to see economic upheaval, governments in collapse, environmental decay, rising crime, disillusioned and disheartened people. Why can't the human race ever live in peace and harmony? Why, with so much abundance are there still so many people who feel empty?

History bears witness to our struggle to find peace, happiness and joy. This struggle has been played out in a myriad of ways. The Industrial Revolution gave us tremendous mechanical capability, but that did not change poverty or social unrest. Next, we looked to science to find the answers to life through physical measuring, trying to verify our reality by quantification. All around we see enormous scientific advances in medicine and technology, but our increased knowledge has yet to solve our problems or elevate the human condition.

In the past fifty years we have seen a vast emphasis on the material. Human consumption and demand for goods are at an all-time high. Having and wanting more has not given people lasting joy or peace. There is still hatred, struggle for power, and wanton waste. Through our lack of awareness, we have even come to the brink of destroying our home, planet Earth.

We have grown in intellect through the ages, amassing knowledge on many subjects, yet we have attained very little wisdom or inner peace. Philosophy, religion, and psychology have fallen short in helping us deal harmoniously and effectively with daily life. Still there is a deep emptiness within many people. This emptiness can manifest itself in overeating, creating debt, joyless relationships, and drug and alcohol abuse, to name a few ways. Despair and chaos are more noticeable today because the sheer number of people intensifies the situation.

Why have we not found the peace and lasting joy that we dearly seek? There are answers to our questions and problems. The answers lie in the voluntary evolution of the consciousness of each individual. A new order and attention to life has to happen to reverse the downward spiral. To create the massive outer changes we all want, we first have to start living life from a more evolved, higher awareness. Through individual effort tremendous changes in the whole structure of life on this planet can occur. As more and more individuals evolve and change, their evolution will effect the entire planet!

This book is a study of life and its different realities. It presents a very down to Earth, grounded approach for the individual who is ready to live life with greater love, purpose, and awareness. The teachings and truths in this book can benefit anyone, but only a person who is ready and whose consciousness is open to change and growth can receive its wisdom.

Knowing Truth

Please use this book as a tool and a guide for your spiritual, emotional, and personal growth. The ultimate authority on what you need in your life or what is true in the universe has to come from within the depths of your own being. People and books can only help reveal the truth. If something has value or is real for you, you will KNOW it. You will not require someone to tell you it is true. The reason I have put the chapter on responsibility first is because this whole book is based on your willingness to find out through your own experience if what I am saying is true or not. You can choose to become more responsible for your life...or not.

The teachings in this book help delineate ways for you to do this, but only by taking action will you know if what I am saying is true.

The "knowing" I am talking about goes beyond an intellectual understanding. It is the way in which you connect to yourself as an all-knowing, spiritual being. That connection may not be readily apparent every day, but when you get "feelings" or awareness of knowing for no particular reason, then realize you have tapped into your higher self. Higher growth and awareness are achieved when you are your own authority. If you constantly do things, even good things, because others tell you to or because you feel you "should" or "ought to," you have relinquished your free will.

Living life with full consciousness should be everyone's goal, because the more you live life with this deep awareness, the deeper connection you make to your higher self as Soul. You are not a body that has a Soul, you are Soul having an Earthly experience. The spiritual part of yourself as Soul is filled with love, joy, and freedom. Living consciously helps you connect with your true self as Soul.

Living consciously with spiritual freedom does not mean rebelling against what other people have taught you for the sake of rebelling. What I am saying is that most of us have relinquished responsibility for our individual lives to others. Most of us have not let ourselves find a way of life or teaching that truly creates value and positive change. It's important to ask yourself if what you are being taught is something you want. If you don't, you are, in fact, giving up personal responsibility. Living unaware or unconsciously, in essence, is living life as a robot.

True Responsibility

The reason people live unconsciously is because on some level they don't want to take responsibility for ALL of their lives. Oh, most of us are willing to take care of the day-to-day responsibilities, and most of us do the best possible job. We see to it the bills are paid and the house is clean and we go to work on time. We get caught up in daily routine. We forget, or we just don't realize, that responsibility on Earth is more than taking care of the human body and making it through the day. As a human being, your true purpose is to become aware of all aspects of yourself and live consciously with this awareness. Your life is actually a spiritual experience. The more you live your life unaware of this, the less benefit you get from this lifetime. True responsibility is living this awareness on every level of your being — your mind, body, emotions, and Spirit! With this kind of awareness comes an indestructible knowing. You can stay centered in joy, love, and purpose no matter what life dishes up.

Most people are not happy or content. They feel empty, without purpose, and do not know why. Yet most people don't want to explore the greater depths of life or their own being to search and find the answers. Society has taught us to seek the quick fix or the "magic pill" philosophy for too long. Contentment and happiness can be achieved only when individuals awaken to their true purpose, connecting to their true selves as Soul. Even if you have acquired great wealth, healed your inner child, and consistently think positively, there will still be an inner yearning to know why you were born and what happens after physical death.

Conducting sessions with thousands of people over the years, I have seen that most people willingly or unwillingly live as victims. Victims do not take full responsibility for their lives. They live as children, unconsciously ignorant of the laws that govern life, caught up in what they want when they want it, with no thought to the consequences of their actions. As with children, it doesn't mean they are bad; it is just that they don't know any other way to be.

I believe until you grasp the truth of life and *live* this truth daily, you are living less of a life. When you are not consciously living each day (or at least trying to live) in union with Spirit, your highest self (Soul), and God, your life is less fulfilling than it could be.

It's possible to come to a deeper understanding of life either by experience or by evolving through a spiritual practice. The vehicle for your higher awareness will come into your life when you are sincerely seeking change and truth. There is an old saying: "The teacher or teaching arrives when the student is ready." I firmly believe that when you are ready for this new awareness, you will be shown how to proceed.

What Is Life About?

All of life and your individual experiences are here to help you get closer to God. The word "God" may evoke fear, anger, distrust, and myriad other emotions. You may have been raised with the beliefs that the creator of all existence, God, is a judgmental, rule-producing being and that you should feel shamed and guilt-ridden for your very existence. I believe God is LOVE. Because God is love, *when you truly love yourself, you in turn love and serve God.*

Throughout our history, we have limited our beliefs and understanding about God. We have let parents, scholars, and religious leaders dictate our understanding of God. Most of us have abdicated our individual responsibility of knowing about God to these "authorities." You must be your own spiritual authority to grow and live to your full potential.

Choosing How to Live

This life of yours is a lesson in awareness and self-love of the highest order. Your schoolroom is Mother Earth, and the classes are your daily life. Whether you are a housewife, an executive, a rocket scientist, or a prisoner, you have picked that role to help you learn your lessons and evolve as your true self: Soul. The life role you have chosen teaches you something you need to learn. Though each life is so very different, all are perfect. You get exactly what you need to grow to your highest potential. What you get may not be what you consciously want, but your higher self (Soul) knows what experiences you need to attain your highest potential. Through your experiences you can grow and achieve awareness and union with God, *if* you choose to see the higher lessons contained within daily life.

How does this relate to responsibility? As a human being, you are given free will. Each moment, you can choose to live life with responsibility toward your higher good or to live and act as a victim. Victims live life from the belief (conscious or unconscious) that circumstances are out of their control. Victims think they have no power.

Life is a series of lessons to help you grow in love, freedom, and awareness. When you live from your higher nature you choose to learn from your lessons or problems. Victims do not. You are given the right to live in darkness and ignorance or to use all of your energy to get closer to God and Spirit, which is the totality of love, freedom, and bliss. This, in fact, is your true purpose for being alive!

Reading this may bring you to ask questions: Why do some of us live in a free country while others are prisoners or are starving in other parts of the world? Why are some people born healthy and others born with defects? Why is it that when you try to live life with Spirit and God, sometimes your life seems to get worse?

Well, to answer those questions brings us to two very important laws of life. Some of you might not agree with these laws, and that's okay. All I ask of anyone, whether you're working in sessions with me or reading this book, is that you give yourself permission to be open to hearing teachings that may be new to you. Then go within yourself and find out if what I say (or what anything anyone else has to say, for that matter) helps you create value for your life right now. Read this book with your "heart" as well as with your mind, and try to keep both as open as possible.

I also want to point out that when you choose to be on the road to a higher awareness in your life, a teaching may be correct for you for a minute, a day, or a lifetime. You will know when a teaching is correct for you because if it is it creates value in your life. It uplifts your life. It brings you closer to "being" love. A correct teaching will help you become more independent and self-reliant. You will know if a teaching is right for you when it helps you become more balanced, happy, and aware of your true self as Soul. A true teaching helps open your heart fully to Divine Love and Spirit, which are really what life is all about.

As your consciousness grows and changes, what helped you before might not be right for you now; for example, the study habits you used in the second grade may no longer work for you when you go to college.

What you hopefully will understand from this book is that growth, reality, and truth are ever-changing. There are laws and teachings that are constant, true, and correct for you at all stages of your growth, and there are some you will want to discard as your awareness of life grows. As you develop inner wisdom and self-discernment, you will know what is valuable for your life in the present moment.

You must control your own life. Only you can know what is necessary for your next step in growth. If at times you are unsure, you will gain wisdom only by doing for yourself. Nobody can live your life for you. No one can tell you what is inside your heart or what you need next for your growth as an individual or as truest self — Soul.

It would be difficult to understand how to live life with total responsibility without understanding two major principles — Cause and Effect, and Reincarnation.

Cause and Effect and Reincarnation

Cause and Effect, simply stated, means that for whatever action you take in your life, you will receive a condition or result because of that action. Actions are thoughts, words or physical deeds; they can be positive or negative. The more positive actions you make, the more positive your life becomes. Negative actions create negative results. Positive actions create value for you and all of life; negative actions devalue you or life in some way. Cause and Effect governs this plane of existence, just as gravity is still present and working in this physical dimension whether you are aware of it or not. The more you live your life consciously, aware of Cause and Effect, the more control you will have to create your life the way you want it to be, while at the same time creating value for the whole of life.

Reincarnation means each Soul is born into a plane of existence to learn the lessons it needs to know to grow in its awareness and union with God. Each individual Soul usually needs more than one lifetime of experience. This is because there is so much to learn about the aspects of Divine Love,

Spirit, and God.

Cause and Effect and Reincarnation are closely tied together. The actions you make influence and create your future. The moment called "now" literally creates your future in this life as well as influences your next life. What actions you have made in the past (in this lifetime or another) have effected your present.

Cause and Effect and Reincarnation clearly explain why some people are born handicapped and some people are not. They explain why some people are born in countries that control freedom and why some are born in countries that uphold an individual's rights. Apparent discrepancies in life are the result of previous actions in other lifetimes. The results surface as accumulated positive or negative effects, or "karma." Karma, a word of Buddhist and Hindu origins, is a name for the results of all the actions we have ever made from the very beginning of our existence.

Karma

A person will receive what is right and deserving, though a person may not necessarily get back the specific effect from someone or something in the past. Karma is exacting; in other words, people receive what they deserve, based on their past actions. For example, your control of another person in a former life could come back to you as the "same" person you controlled now controlling you in this life. Or, the same lesson could surface as a new person or circumstance controlling you. Your lessons can take a hundred scenarios, but the essence of the lesson would be exact. This is how I interpret karma.

Remember, karma can be positive or negative, depending on your actions. An example of positive karma can be something good happening in this life, like being born in a free country or into a wealthy family. Negative karma could be a child born with a defect. With these examples, somewhere in the past, positive and negative effects were accumulated and the results are manifested in this lifetime.

All your experiences and karma can help bring about your deeper connection to Divine Love. The more you view life not as a series of problems but as a series of learning experiences, the faster and more spiritually evolved you become.

Life is eternal, and it may take a while for your negative karma to catch up with you. This is the reason why many people seem to "get away with murder." They really don't; it just seems that way because of the lag in time for repayment. Effects from a former life may not manifest until this lifetime or another. By the time the results of your past actions manifest, you won't remember why they are happening. You don't remember that maybe in the past you weren't all that kind or glorious a person. We have all done things in former lives we would be ashamed of in this life. We also have done many wonderful and loving things. Just remember, whatever is manifesting in your life or mine, you and I have acted to create these experiences, good or bad. This is true whether you remember what you did to create these circumstances or not.

You, as Soul, need all kinds of experiences to grow in knowing God. We all have free will to make choices in each moment. No matter what your past was like or what you may have done, what really counts is the moment, the ever-present "now." It is only in the "now" that you have the power to change. The more you live your daily life with awareness of the incredible power in each of your moments and align your consciousness and actions with Spirit and God, the higher and faster you will evolve. **You can dispel negative karma in the present moment only. You do this by aligning your actions to**

the highest purpose of life. As you consciously increase and use this understanding, you become more attuned to Divine Will, which is pure Divine Love. At the same time, you create a more positive future for yourself.

My Story

Now let me tell you how I came to believe in this way of thinking and how these beliefs have affected my own life. I come from an upper middle-class family. My father owned his own business and I am the youngest of eight (yes, count 'em, eight) children. Needless to say, my parents were Catholics and we were all raised strictly Catholic.

Please understand, I am NOT preaching for or against any belief or faith. I firmly believe whatever path or religion you are practicing is perfect for you now. It is also perfect for you now if you are not currently practicing any formal religion. If you choose to relinquish a certain belief, that doesn't make your former belief bad or wrong, it just makes it not right for you now. In my personal road to growth and awareness I have practiced and tried different religions and beliefs. These have been good for me and my awareness at the time I held them. And when I lived my life with no formal religion and just observed life, that too, was perfect and invaluable. All my experiences helped me grow. Life is your teacher. All of life's answers are within yourself. Every experience is your teacher, when you let the teaching into your consciousness.

Early Childhood

I grew up in what is now called a dysfunctional home, though at the time none of us knew a name for it. I always thought something was strange and off-kilter in the way my family related, because no one in my family talked about feelings. I always felt incredibly alone.

My world and my family's world evolved around my mother's constant illnesses. From my first remembrances of her until her death when I was twenty-three, I never saw her well or happy. She had breast cancer when I was just five. At that time, the treatment for breast cancer was extremely brutal. Her chest was totally scarred from the operations and she had no breasts or nipples. She also had to have intense radiation treatments. The radiation left her skin red and raw and her energy totally drained. The amounts of radiation she received would never be given now. Throughout my childhood, my mother was in and out of hospitals almost every year. She had one kidney removed, her thyroid removed, a hysterectomy, and all her teeth taken out. Needless to say, she was always in pain. Because of the intense pain from the cancer, her doctors prescribed morphine, and she became addicted. I remember one night — I think it was around dinnertime — when she started to go into convulsions. I was very young and truly petrified by what I witnessed. My mother started gagging on her own tongue and she was unaware of what was happening to her. Everyone was racing around trying to help, and I was sent to my room. I remember my sister Judith telling me to pray for her. I thought my mother was going to die, but she didn't. This was just another "normal" occurrence in our household. This kind of drama was always being played out in our house.

That event would be traumatic for any child, but no one in our house talked to me about my mother's illness. We never discussed the traumas or problems our family experienced. When I look back on my childhood, the thing I remember the most was being terribly lonely. I felt lonely because there was no one for me to talk over my thoughts with and no one to listen to me. I had no emotional connection to anyone. I especially felt the loss of not being listened to, because I was the "baby" of the family, and who listens to the youngest child? Ironic, isn't it? I come from a family of eight children, ten people including the adults, and I felt lonely *all* the time. This lack of communication is very normal for dysfunctional families.

Dysfunctional Families

People in dysfunctional families are taught directly and indirectly not to communicate deep feelings and to lock those feelings away and not let them surface. You are taught to bury your head in the sand, to deny your reality because reality is too scary. So it becomes easy to deny the truth of your pain. What is truly crazy or unbalanced in a dysfunctional home life is thought to be "normal." As John Bradshaw teaches so well in his book *Home Coming*, you are taught consciously or unconsciously to view yourself as a mistake or unworthy. When adults come from dysfunctional backgrounds, they haven't gotten the message from their upbringing that they were loved unconditionally. They did not get the proper nurturing so that they, in turn, could learn to love themselves. Little children need love and a healthy self-esteem mirrored back to them from their environment, which includes parents and other members of the family, in order to feel love and self-worth.

Children in dysfunctional homes have been brought up to nurture their parents and deny their own feelings. This lack of positive, healthy mirroring creates shame and feelings of worthlessness. These feelings stay inside the little child who then becomes the wounded adult, until these feelings are faced and processed healthily. (Some ways to help yourself process your feelings healthily are explained later in greater detail.)

The majority of us, if not all of us, come from some kind of a dysfunctional home. A dysfunctional home can be a household of little or no emotional involvement, sexual abuse, heavy criticism, drug and/or alcohol abuse, physical and/or emotional abandonment, or tremendous sickness, as in my family. What characterizes a dysfunctional home is any kind of environment that creates in a person a conscious or unconscious feeling of self-hate, worthlessness, or guilt, just for being. The dysfunctional person sees himself or herself as "less than" and different than other people. You may feel like you don't belong anywhere or you may feel like a mistake.

Unknowingly I grew up hating myself and feeling totally worthless. I felt isolated and different from other people. Unconsciously, I was terribly angry toward my mother for not nurturing me, and I felt tremendous guilt for being so angry toward her. It was a perpetuating cycle of self-hate. I never realized any of these feelings consciously until I was in my mid-twenties.

Most of the clients I see come from dysfunctional homes. And most of the people coming from these situations don't understand their feelings or why they make the choices they make. What happens is that all the negative unconscious beliefs created from their childhood effect their daily lives now. They are constantly carrying in their hearts all the hurt and neglect from their upbringing.

My Mom and Dad

During my upbringing, my mother not only was sick all the time, but she was also addicted to Valium and alcohol. I remember times I'd come home from school and she'd be upstairs and I'd be downstairs and I'd hear a "thud." The thud was her falling to the floor; the Valium and alcohol had caused her to lose her balance.

My mother couldn't emotionally be there for me or anyone else in my family. I know she loved me and she was a good person, but this didn't change the realities of our family life and what was missing in my upbringing as a child. As a child my emotional self never got the love or nurturing I so dearly needed to grow to be a fully functioning, healthy adult.

My brother Michael and I were most affected by her incapacitation because we were the last of the children living at home. When I was in elementary school, my other brothers and sisters were out of the house and my father was absorbed in his business. When he'd come home at night, usually very late, he would retreat, read his business magazines, or go to bed. I don't ever remember him asking me what I did in school that day or if I had any problems. I never remember him listening or relating to me on the emotional level I needed.

Everyone outside the family loved him. To them he was a real outgoing guy, always very positive and enthusiastic. He was definitely enthusiastic, the opposite of my mother. My mother was negative, unhappy and physically weak. My father looked twenty years younger than his actual age. He was very healthy and strong, and always tried to be positive. As positive as he appeared, he never showed his heart to me. Though I loved my father, I could never communicate deeply with him and I never felt him try to connect to me as a person. I could not imagine going to him when I was a child, crying and hurt, and him being there for me with tenderness or warmth and making my hurt all better. We got the message in our family that we had to be strong and perfect. Our emotions, if not happy or positive, were a sign of weakness.

My father's attitude of being extremely positive and my mother's focus of the negative were both examples of dysfunctional behavior. My father's dysfunctional behavior was harder to spot, because he hid his real feelings beneath his positive veneer. Both my parents denied their full spectrum of feelings. Consequentially, my parents' behavior traits were passed down to some degree to and my siblings and me.

I chose to emulate my father's behavior because, outwardly, he looked like a survivor. All I saw in my mother's life was pain, misery, and death. The choice, albeit unconscious, was easy for me: life or death. I chose what I perceived was life. In choosing my father's way of dealing with life, I stuffed all anger, sadness, and loneliness deep inside myself. I would allow myself only to be strong and show strength. And the only way I could communicate to others was on a superficial level. I wore the perpetual "happy face" for society, but I was dying inside!

In my home I was designated the caretaker, and I was excellent at my job. From the time I was around nine or ten years old, I took care of our big house. I did the cleaning, the laundry, the grocery shopping, and the cooking, and I took care of my mom.

My mother was not a total invalid, but she was very depressed and physically worn down from all her operations. What she did most of the time was sit and watch television and smoke cigarette after cigarette. Or she would read for hours and smoke cigarette after cigarette. She was a champion worrier! If there was nothing to worry about she'd invent something. When she was younger, before I was born, she was quite athletic. I was told she often went hunting and hiking with my father. She loved to swim and was an excellent diver, and she taught most of us how to dive. In her younger days, she had a zest for life and communication. My mom was even a member of a club called the Jabberwocky Club, because she and my aunts loved to talk so much. But I never saw that side of her. I never saw her well. I hardly ever saw her laugh.

I got to be an expert at denying my feelings. As I was growing up, my pet cats gave me comfort and a feeling of intimacy, that I missed from my mother and family. Through playing with the cats and taking care of them, I learned a lot about love and affection. They were my friends. I think my connection to them saved me emotionally.

Teenage Years

As I approached my early teens, things went from bad to worse. I saw one of my sisters have a nervous breakdown; she couldn't talk for several days. My father had a nervous breakdown, and my mother went off several times to mental health facilities for weeks at a time. Most of the time I was this little numb body, walking around too scared to feel or talk. I looked up to my older brothers and sisters, yet I felt so isolated from them. I was too young to be included when my brothers and sisters were doing something, and our age differences seemed much more pronounced when we were growing up. In our family there is an age span of fifteen years from myself to the oldest child.

How I Channeled My Beliefs

Nobody talked about anything or discussed feelings. Everything was always "fine." Through all this confusion I was stuffing my feelings more and more, and the need to gain some semblance of control in my life became more paramount. I became bulimic at age thirteen and stayed that way for fourteen years. It just happened. I still don't know how, but it did. I do believe it was a way my unconscious mind helped me survive and control my feelings. It was a way for me to process my

unconscious self-hate and anger. On a scale of one to ten, if ten
was the worst bulimic you could be, I was probably an eight or
nine. By the time I was fifteen, I was throwing up four or five
times a day. Back then no one knew of or talked about this disorder, so I thought I was absolutely crazy. But I told no one, and
I felt powerless to stop. It was a powerful addiction, not unlike
drugs. I remember thinking I would have rather been a prostitute than do this disgusting thing each day. (Being a prostitute
in a good Catholic family, to me, was about the worst thing you
could be. That's how bad I felt about being me.) I had no control over bulimia, and I felt completely worthless.

When I was fourteen, I started drinking heavily and I
would get totally drunk on weekends. I would fast all day, and
then at night I would chug three cans of beer, enough to get
me thoroughly drunk. I started to smoke cigarettes and mari-
juana at fifteen.

I also tried to kill myself twice, once consciously and once
unconsciously. Repressing all my feelings was taking its toll!
My two incidences of attempted suicide occurred at fifteen. At
that time my mother was really dependent on me. She had no
one else with whom to relate, and she used me to vent all her
frustrations. Unconsciously, she was using me to nurture her
emotionally. She'd be yelling at me all the time. I had heavy
responsibilities, but my parents didn't balance my responsibilities with social activities. I had to argue and fight for any normal teen fun. I was really made to feel guilty for wanting to
spend time to enjoy life and have fun or friends.

For a time, my father must have seen what all this tension
was doing to me, because he let me live at a girlfriend's house
for about a month while I recuperated from mononucleosis.
During my stay, I saw what a normal family life was like. The
people who let me stay with them were great. They talked to

their kids and related to their lives. I got to feel what it was like to be loved openly and completely.

They had seven kids living in a little house with one bathroom. I felt more peace and relating going on there than I ever did at my house. I never wanted to go back home. One night my girlfriend and I got drunk. It was a very cold winter night in upstate New York. All my feelings that had been hidden in my heart started to surface, and most were feelings of hopelessness.

That night I felt so bad about my life that I started banging my head against the wall of their family room after drinking a copious amount of alcohol. Her parents were gone, and I was definitely out of control. I then tried to run outside and freeze myself, remembering something my mother told me when I was little. She told me people die in the snow because it is easy to fall asleep and freeze to death before they wake up. I thought that sounded like a painless way to go. I knew, being so drunk, I could fall asleep without too much effort. But my friend was fortunately able to stop me and calm me down.

Depths of Despair

My self-depreciating behavior was not new; I had been thinking about suicide on and off for several years. On previous occasions, I would take out the butcher knives and look at them and wonder how it would feel to stab myself or cut my wrists. I was also leaving lots of little doodles on paper about death and killing myself. One day my brother Robert saw some of these, and he brought them to my mother's attention. But she never talked to me about those cries for help, and I continued to think of killing myself.

Another time I almost died was when my boyfriend invited me to his junior prom. I was a sophomore in high school at the time, and going to the junior prom was a big deal. Well, we went to the dance and had dinner, double-dating with another couple. The other boy was in college, and he invited us to his dorm to drink after dinner. Of course I said yes, and off we went. I always chugged my drinks very quickly, so I could get roaring drunk. I drank about a quart of whiskey sours and a bottle of champagne, and in no time I was unconscious — for at least six hours. They called in a medic at one point because I had stopped breathing. My date had to carry me out of the dorm. As he was carrying me, I was screaming at the top of my lungs, "Help me, help me." Because I was unconscious, I didn't remember a thing.

When they dropped me off at my house at five in the morning, I still couldn't see straight. My mother never noticed or even commented on my torn and vomit-stained dress. I literally crawled up the stairs to my bed. Nothing was ever said about that incident. My cry for help went unnoticed!

But something snapped in me shortly after that night, and I knew I wanted to live. I also knew if I stayed at home I wouldn't survive, so I ran away. I had thought about running away from home since I was eight, and I constantly talked about it to my girlfriend. Then one weekend, I packed some clothes in a paper bag and I took the bus to my oldest brother's house in the city.

Being the ever-responsible person I was, I called my parents and told them where I was. While I was talking to them and trying to explain why I had to leave, the phone was on my knee and I was shaking so much from fear and nerves that the phone almost crashed to the floor, but all I felt was numbness. A short time later, my brother gave me two weeks to find another place to live. He never explained why he kicked me out to find a place of my own. I had just turned sixteen!

My Awakening

I was totally on my own. My parents didn't give me money or emotional support. My brothers and sisters were wrapped up in their own dysfunctional stuff and weren't available to support me in any way either. I was absolutely, totally alone. It was the loneliest time of my life! I felt abandoned by the whole world, but I still wanted to live and find happiness.

What saved me was the realization I was responsible for my life. I started finding answers to my life and life in general. I had always been a deep-thinking child, even as far back as the second grade.

I realized somehow that I had created these awful experiences in my life. Reading books about self-help and self-awareness helped me clarify how and why I had experienced what I had. Spiritually contemplating life gave me inner strength to help dig myself out of the cesspool I was in. I really felt life came down to two choices: To kill myself directly or indirectly, which meant living my life as a victim, or to be in charge of my life and become happy. I chose to take charge.

Understanding Free Will

I learned we are born into circumstances that help us grow; present-life circumstances are results of past actions, which are perfect tools for us to use for self-discovery and growth. When I read these books, the teachings resonated with something in my own being and I just knew what they were saying was true. Knowing this consciously gave me hope and the tools to radically change my life for the better.

You always have free will to live your life the way you want, whether you are aware of this fact or not. Only when you live your daily life from the consciousness of total responsibility do freedom and love fully emerge in your life and heart.

I think the hardest thing for anyone to accept is the understanding that we created all the circumstances in our lives, whether we are happy or unhappy about them. When I understood this truth — when I really got that truth—it changed my life forever. I was ecstatic, because I realized if I had created all the misery in my life, then I have the power to change it. I finally had hope. I knew I was no longer at the mercy of circumstances. I have the power to control my life!

Most people lose hope and joy because they feel powerless to change anything in their lives. I know when I teach this spiritual principle to my clients, the ones who accept it and **LIVE** it change the most and the quickest.

When you live life with the realization that you can consciously be the master of your life, you can then take your life where you want it to go. The key to any change on this planet is incorporating truths into daily life and living those beliefs, not just having an intellectual understanding of them. When you take the teachings of this book and use them, they work. If you read this book and store this knowledge without using it, like so much accumulated mental garbage, then you may be keeping yourself a victim. **Intellectual understanding is NOT the same as action**.

Simply realizing that in each moment I create my future with all my present actions brought me through some of the worst times in my life. I came out of those times stronger, happier, and wiser. In the darkest of times I *knew* my actions made a difference in my life. I kept making my actions positive and value-creating. I knew in my heart, even if I couldn't immediately see the results I wanted, that results were being created on some level in my life. And eventually the results would manifest on the physical level.

Some people have to be in the dumper before they allow

themselves to see a truth or live a truth. That was the case in my life. If I hadn't had the pain and struggles in my earlier life, I don't think I would have pursued the deeper truths of life and God.

No matter where you are in your life or what is happening, it is up to you to take responsibility for the outcome of your life experience. It's what you do **NOW** that counts. This is truly living life responsibly. Find out for yourself how your actions can change your life.

Truth is not someone telling you something is this way or that way. Truth needs to be experienced, and it's up to you to experience it. And for that to happen, you have to be responsible and put these or other teachings that resonate truth for you into action. Responsibility is a partner with action. If you get nothing else from this book, I hope you understand the **actions of your thoughts, emotions, and physical being are actually creating your life.** For you to create the life you want, absolutely know you can change anything you want in your life. You have created all that is in your life now. You can now be a conscious director of your life and create it any way you dream is possible! Responsibility from this perspective is freedom to be your best possible you!

CHAPTER TWO

Beliefs

The time has come
in one man's Soul,
to start his journey
on the road to know...

Step by step she goes
forward, forward, ever forward;
seeing now what she didn't before
reality always present...

New worlds greet him
with open arms
all rejoicing that he has come,
for the worlds have always been there,
waiting...

In her amazement she is confused,
for what she left she thought was the truth.
As she allows the new world to filter through,
more and more she sees the new view...

Nothing has ever been hidden before
he just never traveled this far, was all,
For the new worlds are there for all to see
manifested only for those who believe!

B ELIEFS

There are still many mysteries to life. I believe we are evolving into to a new age of human consciousness! During the last century there has been a reawakening of awareness regarding the power of thoughts and how they affect our lives. Many of us have accepted different ways of perceiving the power of our own thoughts. Beliefs about life, what life is and how it can work have changed.

In this chapter I cover what beliefs are, how they are created, and how you can create more of what you want in your life by harnessing the power of your thinking. The *advanced* beliefs you need to create for a more profound way of living are also discussed.

Thoughts and Energy

Over the last fifty years more and more people have been exposed to the concept that thoughts and beliefs create reality. Beliefs are thought patterns the mind uses to communicate to you and others in this physical universe. Thoughts, no matter how small, are ways in which your mind communicates with you and your environment. These thoughts and beliefs are forms of energy. For the rest of this chapter, the words "thoughts" and "beliefs" mean the same thing.

Thoughts are like magnets, and they are the building blocks to larger beliefs. An analogy for this is how you use words to express yourself. Each word means something, and each word is a building block to a larger communication. When words are put together in an order, as in a sentence, the communication is clearer and deeper than just a single word or phrase. Complex communication, then, is more than single words; it is sentences, paragraphs, or even books.

It is similar with your beliefs. You have many thoughts running through your mind all the time. Your individual thoughts are building blocks to larger, more complex beliefs, which are usually found in your unconscious mind. Your thought patterns bring you to what you consistently and completely believe. The more complex or deeply held your belief is, the harder it usually is to change.

Thoughts are really just different forms of energy. They only seem different than solid things because they have different densities. Besides communication, Soul uses your thoughts, through the use of your mind, to help you create on the physical level. Einstein observed that energy is neither created nor destroyed, it just changes form. Everything is created from energy! Just as radio waves are always in the atmosphere to be received whether you have your radio on or not, your thoughts, too, are always transmitting to life, and consequently they are always creating. Whether you are conscious of your beliefs or oblivious to what you are holding in your mind, your thoughts consistently affect your life. Your life is truly a mirror of what you believe!

What you think and believe determines how you see and interact with life. Your thoughts or beliefs are windows of awareness. If your window is only so big, then you believe that is the only reality. If your window is bigger, you see a bigger picture, or a new aspect to your life. At any point in time, you may feel a particular window is the true aspect of your life, a true representation of reality. Each time you gain in awareness, your belief about what is true about life changes. This is because your window of reality has changed. **Reality is**

actually a point of perception of consciousness.

It's like the story of the three blind men. They stood by an elephant and tried to describe it. Each man felt the part of the elephant closest to him. One felt the eyes, one the elephant's tail, and the other the elephant's leg. Each felt something true about the elephant. But they had only part of the truth, because their windows of reality (their experiences) were different. What they perceived (or were conscious of at the time) was only part of the truth.

In your life you are like those blind men. You may be blinded to the greater truths of life or limit yourself in what you can achieve by the thoughts you hold. Many people want to change some aspect of their lives, but they don't want to alter their attitudes, thoughts, or actions to accomplish this. A great part of changing your reality entails changing *what* you believe.

The Mind

People get caught in the trap of the mind and become lazy when it comes to changing their attitudes and beliefs. Change requires effort, and changing your beliefs about yourself and the world around you necessitates focusing your thoughts consistently on your goal or objective. It means being open to different ways of thinking and attitudes, and releasing old patterns that no longer serve you. It means giving yourself the freedom to pick and choose the beliefs that will add the most value to your life. When you live with the flexibility of choosing your beliefs, you can indeed change your life.

Realize that the mind is the seat of your thoughts. Your mind is very much like a computer terminal. It is not intelligent by itself; it is the vehicle by which your thoughts are transferred to the physical plane of existence through Soul. Soul is the actual power behind your thoughts. Without Soul, which is your true self, your body wouldn't be able to move or think.

True power comes from Spirit. Humans, especially now, seem to worship the intellect as the ultimate power. Actually, the intellect is a limited tool used by Soul to function in this dimension. The mind is physical, and its capacity is limited. Anything physical is intrinsically limited.

Only Soul or Spirit is limitless. Soul is "above" the mind and the negative patterns that have been created there. Too many of us try to solve problems with intellect alone. No matter how intelligent you are, there comes a time when intellect will fail to conquer your problems. Ultimately, you have to tap into the power of Soul to completely transcend the erroneous or limiting patterns of your mind.

Parts of the Mind

Understanding how your mind works is enormously important in helping change negative beliefs, and it is one of many tools to help you grow and change. Knowing the basics of how your mind works can help you discover your beliefs and how they are limiting your life.

The mind is composed of the conscious and the unconscious. The conscious part of your mind is the seat of logic and reason. The unconscious mind is the seat of habits and behaviors, and it is the true powerhouse of the two.

When you are born, you use your unconscious mind almost exclusively. Your conscious mind (logic and reason) doesn't become fully formed until you are about seven years of age. From birth to seven, you absorb beliefs about yourself and your environment directly into your unconscious mind. During your early, formative stages there are no boundaries between you and your environment. The people and things around you seem like parts of you. In your mind, when you are a small child, there is no separation between you and others. So whatever you experience from others, you unconsciously believe is part of you. I call this "developmental mirroring." Your beliefs, then, are formed through the mirroring you received from your parents, family members, school, and television — all your life experiences. You grow up thinking of these beliefs as ultimate truth.

You are very impressionable in those early years. For example, if your parents had low self-esteem, they could have passed that belief on to you by how they took care of you, how they felt about themselves, and the examples they set. You were receptive to the emotional and mental energy around you as well as how you were physically treated. As a child, if the energy of the people around you was negative or self-abasing, your unconscious mind picked up the belief that *you were* not worthwhile. Those early beliefs formed a window of what you felt was real or not real. You took this reality into adulthood and made actions based on your beliefs.

Look at this scenario: If you were raised in India, your perception of life would be vastly different than if you were raised in the United States or Japan. None is wrong or right, it's just a section of all reality.

The mind is very much like a computer — it runs from the data that is entered. The computer doesn't question the logic or reason of the data, it just responds. The unconscious mind runs on the input it receives without questioning if the material is positive or not. Your unconscious mind has been programmed since birth, and it will continue to run on these programmed beliefs until you change them. Your unconscious mind is something like 88% of your total mental power. It is much more powerful than the logical, conscious part. Think of your unconscious mind as big, dumb, and extremely powerful.

On the other hand, your conscious mind functions from logic and reason. Though this part is only 12% of your mental power, you can direct your thinking to help your unconscious mind create healthy and value-creating beliefs.

Once your unconscious mind is programmed, you attract experiences and people into your life in accordance with the beliefs you hold. Thoughts, being energy, vibrate at certain rates of speed, and those vibrations attract like vibrations. This is how you attract to you what you believe. You actually unconsciously draw into your experience that which you hold to be true. **Truths or beliefs are only relevant to your capacity to be aware.** For example, as a child you may have grown up believing in Santa Claus. That was your truth or reality. As you grew in consciousness and knowledge of life, your awareness changed and you were able to incorporate a new set of beliefs about Santa. Your capacity to see new dimensions of life expanded, and this growth in awareness helped you change your belief about what is true or real.

Examining Beliefs

On this planet, you react to and live from what you believe. You cannot get away from your beliefs. Every thought is a belief; if you have a mind, you will have beliefs! This is how everyone functions in this dimension. **The key to your growth and happiness is what you choose to believe.** Because you control your thoughts (your beliefs), you therefore control your realities. No one pours thoughts into your head or tells you to think this or that. You are in total control of your life, but you may choose not to exercise this control, or you may be unaware you even have this control.

Most people will tell you that they believe something when they see it, but in truth it is the exact opposite. Your reality is a reflection of your beliefs! If you were raised with the belief money is the root of all evil, then the likelihood of your accumulating wealth is slim, until you change your belief. You may consciously want more money, but until you change your unconscious beliefs regarding money, you will not achieve your goal. This is true with every aspect of your life, from your health and relationships to your beliefs of what you think is right or wrong.

How do you recognize what beliefs you are holding in your unconscious, the hidden part of your mind? You can identify your unconscious beliefs by the circumstances and situations that are in your life now. For instance, if you want to lose weight and haven't been able to, then somewhere in your unconscious is a belief or set of beliefs that counter your conscious desire. If you want a positive relationship and you continue attracting inappropriate people, then you can be sure you are holding beliefs in your unconscious mind that are keeping you from this goal. Know that circumstances in your life mirror your inner, unconscious beliefs about yourself.

Let's look at this example. Lisa came to me because she wanted to make more money. When she came to me she was making more money and had more friends than ever before, but she wanted to make even more money and have her business grow even larger. During Lisa's session, I asked her if she had any conscious beliefs that she would be lonely or people wouldn't like her if she became more successful. What we discovered was that Lisa *consciously* felt comfortable with success and money.

Her conscious mind, the one with logic and reason, was in perfect accord with what she wanted. Even though she felt there were no unconscious beliefs holding her back, Lisa still couldn't get beyond a certain income.

Hypnosis, which I incorporate into my clients' sessions, is a powerful tool for reaching the unconscious mind. During a session, I suggested to Lisa's unconscious mind that she release any beliefs through her morning dreams that kept her from making more money. (Dreams, as you will learn, are messages from your deeper unconscious self or from your truest self, Soul.) The next week, she came in with a dream that symbolized her unconscious beliefs. Lisa saw herself at a fair with lots of people. In the middle of the fair was a very tall ladder. She started to climb the ladder. At the top was a box, and she found herself alone at the top. This dream symbolized her deeper feelings about success and money. It said she'd be alone if she were successful. Her unconscious beliefs were in direct conflict with her goal and conscious beliefs. Unconsciously, Lisa was afraid of being alone at the top! Based on the dream, we worked on changing the unconscious beliefs that were keeping her from growing her business and in just a few months her income had doubled!

Circumstances in your life are created by the consistent beliefs your mind holds consciously and unconsciously. Your thoughts are intrinsically a part of Cause and Effect. Consequently, the more pessimistic your thoughts are, the more negative things you will attract to your life. The more your thoughts are evolved or advanced or (better yet) spiritual in nature, the more your life will reflect those beliefs.

Success and Victim Thinking

Very successful people seem to have common beliefs. Successful people and highly evolved people use their thoughts to create the lives they want. They tend to live with a sense of total responsibility for what happens to them. Even when they don't like what they see, successful people realize they can choose to create what is in their lives, and they choose how they react to circumstances. People who are winners and happiest in life tend to believe they have the creative ability to change their lives. Winners refuse to live as victims!

Victims believe they have no power or control over their circumstances. If you feel you are powerless, you proclaim to life, "I am a victim." When you are coming from the powerless victim mode, you attract all the circumstances that reflect being a victim, such as struggle, sickness, poverty, emotional strain, and people who treat you badly.

Both being a winner and being a victim are beliefs. Since you can choose what you believe, why not choose to focus on beliefs that create value instead of suffering?

Always be conscious of your self-talk, the internal dialogue that ceaselessly marches through your head. Focus your self-talk in a direction that creates value for your life.

Because the victim role is easy to get into, you may not always be aware when you are projecting victim-hood into your life by your self-talk. For instance, victims are usually worriers. Victims usually believe if they don't worry, something won't turn out right. In actuality, when you worry you attract what you fear! (Remember, your thoughts are created through Cause and Effect.) By constantly associating something with negative feelings or thoughts, you create a breeding ground for the situation to happen — most probably the very situation you don't want!

When I was a bulimic, I thought constantly about food and my weight. I worried about calories and whether I would gain weight. My obsessing intensified the condition I was afraid of and this thought pattern kept weight on me. There is more to healing bulimia than changing thought patterns, but changing thoughts is a very important part of healing the condition. My

thought patterns when I was bulimic were stuck on the negative. The mind is truly a machine; I turned my machine into a
worry producer and, consequently, a fat producer.

Now, since I've changed those beliefs, I never think about
food until I am physically hungry. My old negative thought
patterns have been changed. I consistently altered my thinking
patterns and based all my daily actions to live life with a higher awareness. I haven't weighed myself since I was twenty-
seven, and I am at least one dress size smaller now than I was
when I was bulimic. Food is no longer a worry for me and I no
longer obsess over it. I can eat anything I want, and I stay at
my perfect weight. I actually eat more now than I did when I
worried all the time about my weight and obsessed over food.

Worry

Worry is a thought process filled with tension. Tension
causes delay in creating what you want, so worrying can actually repel what you desire. Let's say you are a whiz at positive
thinking and you do it all the time. Positive thinking is controlled by the conscious part of your mind. If you have inner
tension when you think those positive thoughts (affirmations),
the true, deep belief in your *unconscious* mind is that you ***don't***
believe you will succeed. ***Tension and worry go hand in hand
with disbelief.***

The true belief you hold when you worry is that the
physical world and all the happenings in it are more powerful
than God and Spirit. You will feel no fear when you are connected to the Holy Spirit! This is a lesson I find myself learning over and over again. When you are relaxed about a particular circumstance, you are positive about the situation and will
draw it to yourself quicker. To achieve change, your conscious
and unconscious minds have to be in alignment.

Tension and worry, though, can help you grow. You can use them to help you discover hidden beliefs that keep you from achieving your goals. When you examine what you are worried or tense about, you discover what your hidden beliefs are.

Being human, it is very easy to fall into a state of fear and worry. For me it has been a lifelong battle against the programming I learned from my mother, who worried for a career. My mind and thoughts are now much calmer. I am more positive and definitely more in control of my thoughts. Now when I fall into fear and worry, I get out of that state much more quickly.

Limitations of Mental Reprogramming

My career as a success coach/hypnotherapist has been devoted to helping people rid themselves of unwanted beliefs. When I started this career, I already knew how powerful thoughts and beliefs could be. I had walked barefoot across red-hot coals unharmed. I had jumped off a forty-foot telephone pole with a broken hand. (I did have a harness, but I still had to battle my fear of heights. I now know that your knees do knock together when you are very afraid!) I had also taken many courses that taught ways to help individuals change negative beliefs. I did these things to prove to myself how powerful the mind and beliefs can be.

I went into my profession expecting to see quicker, deeper and more powerful changes and results with my clients than with traditional counseling or coaching methods, and this has been proven to be true. But I didn't expect to find out the mind is limited in how much it can help you to heal and change. I experienced within myself and with my clients limitations when I used only mental tools to heal negative beliefs.

This is the limitation I see with training or counseling

that focuses solely on mental reprogramming. Initiating changes on all levels helps to create advanced changes within the individual. When I incorporated Spiritual principles into my coaching sessions, my clients achieved greater, more comprehensive advancements. Any good therapist or coach will incorporate principles to help heal an individual's emotions as well as thought patterns. What most therapies or trainings don't do is incorporate Spirit into the healing process.

Spirit is the stuff that makes us...us. You are not a body with a Soul; you are Soul using a body for this physical existence. When you die, it is because Soul has left your body. Without Soul, your body no longer functions, much less thinks. Spirit and Soul are more powerful than your mind, thoughts, and beliefs. It just makes sense to use the highest part of yourself to change your other aspects.

This doesn't mean people who only use mental techniques don't get results. On the contrary, many, many people have grown and changed for the better with mental reprogramming and re-framing. What I am saying is there may come a time when the mental techniques you have used to change your thoughts and beliefs won't work anymore. This is the time to get above the mind by connecting to your Spiritual self. The true power that affects your mind, emotions, and physical body comes from Soul and God.

Throughout this book, there are techniques to help you change all aspects of yourself: emotional, mental, physical, and spiritual. Reading this book and trying to consciously understand and incorporate its teachings into your life will do much to change your beliefs about reality. As your beliefs about reality change, the actions you make with your thoughts, words, and deeds will change. Your environment will then start to reflect those changes as well.

Mass Consciousness Beliefs

All people on this planet send out thought waves of energy. When this energy is focused on the same thought or perceived reality, it is called a mass consciousness belief. This shared reality can be a collective belief of a small group of people or of all the people on this planet. At any given time, a group can share a reality. It is important to be aware of mass consciousness beliefs so that you can exercise freedom of choice. Too many of us lead lives guided by advertising and societal rules instead of individually choosing what is right for our lives. If you don't know you are reacting from a mass consciousness belief, you cannot be in a position to choose what you want to believe. You can only grow as Soul when you are free to be your authentic self, living your life as its creator, not as someone being led.

Living the way you feel is best for you and encouraging change within yourself can be difficult. The more you allow yourself to live based on beliefs that serve your highest good, the more you can create a life that is right for you, not the life someone else wants for you. At times you may be the only one who has the consciousness to live a more advanced way. Because we are social creatures, it can be hard to be different or to be the first to live and act from a different belief.

It takes courage and fortitude to grow and open up to new realities. People of this planet once believed the world was flat; that was the mass consciousness belief of that time. When Christopher Columbus left to sail to India, people thought he was crazy to travel further than was previously known. Most people of his day thought he would fall off the end of the Earth. But he believed the world was round, and he now has a place in history because he literally broadened the mass consciousness belief of his time. He helped change the concept of reality of his world!

Every day, you are faced with mass consciousness beliefs you might take as truth. They are so pervasive you may forget or not even realize you don't have to believe them. These beliefs can be handed down from parent to child (and you don't usually question what you are taught as a child). Many people may still think beliefs they learned as children are the only reality. Many of my clients are amazed when I tell them they no longer have to believe certain "truths" from their past. They come to find out that what they thought was truth was, in reality, a belief they were taught.

One very simple mass consciousness belief I work with all the time is: People always gain weight when they quit smoking. Most of my clients think this is true. Some people do, in fact, gain weight when they quit smoking. But the point is you do not have to gain weight. The weight gain is just a belief. When I quit smoking I decided not to adopt that belief. I actually lost weight when I quit smoking!

Changing Beliefs

People possess beliefs for various reasons. Most people don't realize their beliefs can be changed. Just because you have always believed something doesn't mean you have to believe it for the rest of your life. Just knowing you can believe anything you want is very liberating.

Adopting new beliefs can also be frightening. Lots of people don't want to change their thought patterns because they are afraid of the unknown. Many people are comfortable with what is known to them, even if what is known causes them unhappiness.

People keep beliefs because they don't know how to change their thought patterns. I teach people who are unaware of the nature of their thoughts to become aware of new possibilities. I provide guidance to help them change negative thought patterns, but I cannot help anyone who refuses to change. If you want to change badly enough you will be presented with tools for achieving that change. Whether it is from this book or someplace else, the answers will come to you. Then it is up to you to use them. You are the master of your own destiny. It comes down to what kind of life you want.

Power of Positive Expectation

Here are some basic ways to use thoughts to achieve your goals and desires. One basic belief successful people use to create their goals is the power of positive expectation. Positive expectation is looking forward to success in the future. It is anticipating realized results. Some people expect the positive, while others expect and focus on the negative. You always attract that which you expect! You probably didn't realize you are *always* in a state of some kind of expectation, positive or negative.

When you want to create a new situation for yourself, the likelihood of success is increased by the amount of energy you put into **positive** expectation. Successful people consciously focus on what they want out of life — they fill themselves with positive expectation. Arnold Schwarzenegger is a wonderful example of someone who consciously uses positive expectation. He has said he knew his name would be world known; he *expected* it to happen. By keeping his mind focused on his expectation, he realized his desire. Another shining example of positive expectation is Carol Burnett. Someone once asked her if she expected to be successful as an actress when she first started out. She replied she *always* expected to be successful. Thus, when embarking on new adventures, try to keep your outlook filled with positive expectancy.

Exercise

Learning How to Visualize

One vehicle of positive expectation is using the power of visualization consciously. Whether you are aware of it or not, you visualize everyday. When you daydream about a loved one or where you want to go to dinner, you are actually visualizing. The process can be as simple as filling yourself up with a feeling of what you want to experience, like what you may feel when your are going to meet a loved one. One part of visualizing is the "seeing" part or "imagining" aspect; the other element is the sense or feeling regarding the situation.

The more you use all your senses in visualizing, the more powerful the process becomes. For example, when you imagine where you want to go to dinner, think about how the place looks and the wonderful way the food smells, hear the conversation, and feel the texture of the linen napkin in your hand as you hold it. Create details with your imagination, remembering the sensations from all your senses. This procedure can be done with any aspect of your life.

Now put your visualization in the present moment. Assume you have it now (whatever your particular "it" is). Put your desire in your mind for the good of all and yourself. Then release your attachment (control) to the outcome of your desired objective to Spirit.

Here's another example. Suppose you have always been in a salaried job and you start to seriously think about starting your own business. First, assume you can have your desire. Get as clear as you can about what you want to do. For instance, imagine what kind of people you'd like to work with, the income you'd like to make, if you'd like to travel and so forth.

Next, imagine yourself in the business and use as many senses as possible to make it real to you. Put it in the present moment because your thoughts only create in the now. Be aware if you constantly say to yourself, "I will have this"— with the word "will," you are programming your desire to stay in the future. The future never really comes. There is only the ever present now.

Ask Spirit to send you the perfect business for your growth and happiness and for the good of all. The phrase "for the good of all" is very important because with it you are releasing control over other people or Spirit. When you phrase your desires this way, you are ensuring development from your highest self, and the likelihood of incurring negative karma is lessened.

When you release control of the outcome to the Holy Spirit, you become a partner with Spirit. When you are open this way, Spirit will manifest whatever is necessary for your highest good and the good of all life. The more you trust this truth, the happier you will be. (Your ego, on the other hand, does not always know or care what is for your highest good or the good of others.) Be assured that all things are being brought to you in the quickest fashion and that all creation starts from the inner parts of you, like feelings and thoughts and moves to your outer reality. ↶

Working with Spirit

A great visualization to work with the Holy Spirit is one where you put all your thoughts and feelings about what you want into a pink cloud. Let's say you want a new career. Picture yourself making the amount of money you want and being in the kind of circumstances and with the type people you'd like to be around. Use all your senses. Next, see that cloud rising into the sky with all those feelings, thoughts, and images and see it disappear. The pink represents Divine Love, and the cloud represents the effortless way in which you release your goals to Spirit.

Always do both the inner work and the outer work to manifest anything in your life. After you do your visualizations each day, take actions in your outer life to bring whatever you want (like the new career) into your life while trusting in the power of the Holy Spirit. Try to put yourself in a place where you no longer need or feel anxious about your goal. The more you let go of the feeling of need, the faster things will manifest for you.

Before I started my career, I had a very clear idea: I wanted to work with people and, at the same time, have a business with which I could grow and change. I wanted to be able to make a certain amount of income and I wanted to always love and enjoy my work. I did not ask the Holy Spirit to give me such-and-such business or to take anything away from anyone else. I knew the perfect career would manifest itself (even when there were no visible signs apparent). I held on to the expectation that my perfect business would manifest, and it did. These techniques really work!

Receiving

Something else that can keep you from changing and getting what you want is being blocked about receiving. Anything you want is, in reality, just energy. Thoughts are energy. To grow and change, you must be open to having positive energy enter your life, and you must be aware of letting your old beliefs go so that you are able to *receive* abundance in the form of new, positive, enabling beliefs. The more you are open and receptive, consciously and unconsciously, to beliefs that are in harmony with what you want, the faster you manifest your desires.

To grow fully, you must have a balance between giving and receiving. This balance is really a flow of energy. One basic reason people don't accomplish their goals is that they shut off their abundance. Most people are unaware they don't know how to receive.

If you are constantly making goals about money and you don't acknowledge and accept other forms of abundance, like unexpected help, a gift, or a compliment, you might have a problem with receiving. Spirit, which is total abundance, will only flow to where there is acceptance or openness.

The primary reason for not accepting abundance is the basic belief you are not worthy. This is usually held in the unconscious mind, and you may not even be aware of it consciously. When you feel lovable and worthy, both consciously and unconsciously, you can accept all the good things life has to offer.

Throughout this book, you will find ways to help you live your life from a deeper and more positive place. Beliefs are tools, and you can use these tools in any way you want. You have choices, and you have the power to change. This is the most empowering belief you can consistently hold. *You, as Soul, are limitless!*

CHAPTER THREE

Our True Purpose of Living

Who am I?
Where am I going??
What am I doing???
Not Now!
NOT Me!!
God NOT THIS!!!!
Why me? Why ME? WHY ME???
AARRRRGGGHHHHH!!!!!!!!!!!!!!!!!
I can't STAND IT anymore!!!

Nothing in my life makes any sense............ I guess............
Well,..... I guess I could.
If only I would, If I CHOOSE to
grow myself,
to the highest place
within myself
THEN I could.........
see what it means,
to REALLY be,
ME!

Who are we truly, and what is the reason for our existence? These are not easy questions to answer. Ultimately, you have to answer them for yourself from your own inner searching and *experience* of truth. Truth is to be experienced. It is not accumulation of mental facts.

You As Soul

Simply stated, you are Soul. You are not a body with a soul, you ARE Soul. Soul is a happy, joyful, loving entity. For now, realize that you are Soul and, as Soul, you are an individualized and unique expression of God. We are all part of God.

Most of us were raised with the concept that we are a body that has a soul. In truth, it is the exact opposite. We have a body to give Soul a vehicle to live in this plane of existence, the physical level of being, the planet Earth.

When you live from the perspective that your true self is Soul, then a shift in your awareness occurs. You look at life a little differently and you start to make life choices based on this awareness. The real meaning and purpose of your life starts to peep through your mind and your daily routine takes on new and deeper meaning. The reason most of us don't live from this higher understanding is because we get caught up in the day-to-day routines of living. Concentrating on the mundane physical aspects of life tends to block out knowledge and consistent awareness of God and the spiritual nature and purpose of life. Absorption in daily life can separate you from the knowledge that your true self is Soul. When you live your life from this elevated awareness, you realize you are more than your body, thoughts, or achievements. You are Soul!

Why Is Soul Here?

Why is Soul in a body, and why are you having this life? What does it mean to have an elevated awareness, and what does that elevated awareness have to do with your happiness and your daily life?

Soul uses your body as a vehicle to experience the physical level of existence. (I use the phrase "physical level of existence" because there are many different realities or planes of experience besides the planet Earth.) In essence, Soul is on Earth to learn to become a co-worker with God. Now that may sound like complete drudgery or bring up feelings of oppression to some of you, but the more you unify your purpose with God and Spirit, the more Divine Love you experience and the happier you become. This is because God and the essence flowing from IT (Spirit) is pure LOVE! When you are unified with Divine Love, how can you not be happy, no matter what else is going on?

Living your daily life as a co-worker with God is like being a single drop of water in the ocean. You may only be one drop, but when you unify with all the other waterdrops, you have the strength and power of the entire ocean. The same thing holds true with individual consciousness. When you unify your purpose with that of the Holy Spirit and God, you can eventually have ITS power coursing through you. Separating your purpose or consciousness from that "biggest" reality limits what you can experience and achieve.

Or you can view being a co-worker of God like the Native Americans who saw themselves as intrinsically linked with Mother Earth. They lived in harmony with the laws of nature, and there was peace and harmony to their existence. Being a co-worker with God is simply following the highest and happiest way of living. It is going with the flow of life instead of swimming against it.

You as Soul need many experiences to develop as a co-worker with God, a state where Soul functions from total Divine Love for itself and all of God's creatures. This takes effort on Soul's part and many lifetimes of learning to achieve. When you live as God's co-worker, you realize there is no separation between you, God, and all of life. What you do for others and for yourself does affect the totality of life.

Reincarnation Revisited!

It's hard to further discuss Soul's need for different experiences without explaining reincarnation in more depth. Reincarnation, on the Earth plane, is Soul experiencing different lifetimes by being born again and again into different physical bodies. Through reincarnation, you as Soul gains experiences you need to achieve a greater understanding of God and to develop your capacity for love, wisdom, charity, and service.

Through each incarnation or new lifetime, you (Soul) accumulate a deeper understanding of spiritual principles and you develop your capacity to love and to be a fully conscious part of Spirit. Even though you've had many different lives, both as men and women, Soul keeps its identity intact. When you are reborn, a filter comes over your mind so your past lives are not easily apparent. Otherwise, your present mind would get confused, and not accomplish much of anything in this life.

Starting each lifetime fresh and unaware of previous lifetimes is like starting your day with a fresh attitude. When you start each day as a new beginning, unencumbered by the previous day's happenings, you can make stronger and more positive actions each day. Similarly, as Soul, you start a new life with fresh challenges to spur you on the road to knowing and experiencing God. Hopefully you are accumulating more good karma than bad and, through your experiences, a greater understanding of Spirit with each life. This understanding comes through and helps you develop a more positive life when you live each moment with truth and Spirit to the best of your abilities.

Your Evolution

The example of your growth and development as a human is similar to Soul's own development. You start out as a baby learning how to walk and talk. Then you go to school to learn various subjects necessary for your adulthood. During this time you interact with new people and learn new social skills. Each stage of life teaches you something necessary to help you grow and develop. One level of learning makes way for a more advanced level, and so on. Without your experiences as a baby and a toddler, it would be nearly impossible for you to develop skills necessary for your advancement as an adult.

Soul's reincarnation is a similar process. You as Soul were born from God, and God has placed you on your journey of growth experiences to gain wisdom. God wants you to be happy and for you to be all you can be. Just as a baby is born self-absorbed and innocent of the workings of life, so too is Soul. As individuals need many different kinds of situations to develop into capable adults, so Soul needs these varied experiences of different lifetimes to develop wisdom, love, and compassion for all of life.

"As Above, So Below"

There is an old saying: "As above, so goes below." Change and growth start with higher spiritual knowledge, which filters down to the human state of consciousness. Changes in Soul's development affect all aspects of your daily life now, and, your individual life now mirrors the development from your Soul's previous reincarnations.

Why does Soul therefore travel this route to know God? In the human state of consciousness, there will always be questions that we can't answer. Our world is material, and its nature is intrinsically limited. Neither you nor anyone else will ever know God or the workings of life completely from the intellect. You have to go above your emotions and mind, straight to your true self as Soul, in order for you to realize and fully be connected to God and what life is all about. This is God-Realization.

God-Realization

The state of God-Realization is an elevated state of awareness — a direct knowing and communion with God, the Holy Spirit, or the Totality of Life (whatever you feel comfortable calling IT.) This communion is not achieved with your intellect, but through a direct link as Soul to Spirit. It's achieving and *being* in this state in the human form before you leave your body at death. It's experiencing a little bit of heaven on Earth!

Experiencing heaven on Earth does not mean that you will never experience problems, difficulties, or emotions. God-Realized people look pretty much the same as anyone else, and they tend to all the normal day-to-day stuff that the rest of us do. God-Realized individuals can be laborers or world leaders. What has changed for them is their inner awareness and connection to Spirit. Their intention, direction, and purpose for life has evolved and changed. They are consciously leading lives in harmony with the higher purpose of Spirit and God. And they are doing this with their everyday lives. Their inner joy, happiness, and experience of love is not dependent on what is happening in their outer lives, because they have a direct link with

Spirit, Divine Love, and the truths of life.

To serve God and achieve the higher states of awareness, it is not necessary to separate yourself from friends, family, or the things you love to do. What is necessary is the intention you hold in your heart while you live your life. The more you evolve and the more you consciously live your life in the name of God, the more your life becomes exceptionally meaningful. Anything less is simply mechanical action to cover the wants of your ego and your body. Your ego and your body do end, but you as Soul are immortal. If you live only for the sake of your body or your ego you will find that no true lasting happiness can result! This is true because your focus is on things that have no permanence; your body and ego will one day die, but you as Soul are immortal. This doesn't mean you never do things for your physical self or become a martyr; it means shifting your focus while you live your daily life.

Inner and Outer Self

The key to achieving a truly purposeful, happy life is to consciously dedicate your daily life to this higher purpose — connecting to Spirit in your daily life. Highly Evolved Souls live each moment awakened to Spirit, their inner growth, and their mission or purpose on Earth. Your awakening affects your daily life by the actions you take and from the deep intentions you keep in your heart. This awareness may be with your outer consciousness, in your inner self, or both.

The inner part of a person is unseen, like emotions. The outer part of a person is the physical body and what can be seen with the physical eyes and felt with the other senses. The outer part of life is what most people center on. It's what most people think is the only reality. True happiness and growth are achieved from your inner self, your inner awakening. When you focus on your inner awakening, the inner change that manifests will effect change in your outer life. Change in your outer environment is always preceded by change within your inner self. Your inner self is made up of emotional, mental, and spiritual aspects of yourself.

Soul's Mission

Just as each Soul is different and unique, so too is its mission or purpose. Each Soul has a mission for Spirit and God. When you live your life from your heart dedicated to God or the Divine of Life, all missions are important. Neither is better nor greater than the other. You are willingly led by Spirit, and IT uses you where your talents are needed. You are not giving up your free will or individuality — you realize this is the happiest way to live, and you willingly partake in Spirit's direction. It is similar to floating down a river with the current instead of fighting against it. Spirit is always leading you to your highest happiness and development. Let yourself flow with IT. When you truly understand this, you will happily be led by Divine direction.

To live a fully awakened life, compared to an average life, is like comparing a baby's awareness of itself and life to that of a fully grown adult. The person is the same, but the consciousness is at different stages of development.

The baby is consciously unaware of its surroundings and what life means; the baby reacts and depends on its parents for survival. Babies are limited in their freedom to move, and so they are limited in what they can experience. They view reality in a very different way than fully grown adults do. Both are in the same body and the same world. What has changed is their growth and awareness. Physical, mental, and emotional growth has to take place for the baby to become a fully functioning adult.

To grow as Soul, the same kind of growth has to take place within your consciousness and deep within you. We all have free will to live our lives the way we want. You can choose to allow yourself to mature and grow within your spiritual self, or you can choose not to grow.

If you do choose to grow in spiritual awareness, how do you accomplish this? How do you connect with yourself as Soul to get what you need to grow toward a higher self-realized state of awareness, or God-Realization?

Changing your awareness of life entails knowing where you are now. I tell my clients being aware of obstacles is the first step in growth. It's similar to diagnosing an illness. Without knowing what your illness is, how can you treat it?

Growing As Soul

Your first step, then, in growing as Soul is to acknowledge you are Soul. The next steps are to develop your awareness of truth and Spirit, and then connect to God or the Divine in this lifetime. The more you come from your inner direction to know God and Spirit, the more God and Spirit flows through your being and life.

This desire should not be a whim, where you try on a spiritual principle for a few days or a few months. The desire I am talking about is an ongoing quest; it is changing your perception of what is important in your life and truly understanding that what is real and important is Spirit and Divine Love. The actions you take in your life from that point on will be geared toward knowing greater truths, and your intention will be on incorporating those truths with all of your being into your daily life.

To grow Spiritually means taking complete responsibility for your life. You have in some way, shape, or form created all the happenings in your life. Now it is up to you to create the actions necessary to achieve spiritual growth. No one can grow for you.

Without living responsibly in the most complete sense of the word, you cannot expect to see your life evolve past material consciousness.

Many people have come to me for coaching. The people who grow the most take hold of what I teach and apply it to their daily lives. They are action-oriented people. They work to overcome their problems and achieve their goals. The people who receive minimal or no results from my sessions are those who want me to "fix" them. They will not incorporate their newfound knowledge into their daily lives. They think hearing the answers to their problems will make their troubles go away. No one can fix you or grow for you. You have to fix yourself and be in charge of your own growth.

Many people who search for God and happiness put very little effort into their spiritual selves, choosing instead to put more effort into entertainment and superficialities. They hope God (or someone) will come along and magically change their lives for them. Or they think that if other people would change, then they would be happy, or if a particular circumstance changed, then their lives would have meaning.

Lasting happiness is found by getting a greater connection with your true self as Soul and living out your true purpose. The way to happiness and growth is to develop your spiritual self. This is not done by wishing or hoping but by taking consistent actions. When you do this, your outer world starts to smooth out and become more harmonious and joyful. Difficult circumstances take on a new meaning and purpose when you come from that spiritual sense and awareness. The hard things in life get easier to handle when you live from this perspective.

Religion and Spiritual Practice

The way I have found to connect to my Spiritual self is through spiritual practice. Many people are taught that if they go to church once or twice a week and listen to someone preach, they are taking care of their spiritual development. They may be. But to reach the state of God-Realization, you need a consistent spiritual practice that helps charge and vitalize your life daily. Be honest with yourself about what you are receiving from your present religion or practice. I believe a practice is right for you when you are feeling more filled with joy and love and when you create more value in your daily life because of your spiritual practice. Therefore, how you live and believe is of the utmost, vital importance.

Your religion or spiritual practice should be part of your *daily* life, not just an afterthought you stuff into a little niche in your week. Change and growth occur in the "now." Your religion should help you become more of an individual, help you connect with Spirit now, and recharge your daily life. If your practice, religion, or belief is doing this for you now, great, stay with it. If it does not, give yourself the permission to practice the religion or belief that honors your self, Spirit, and Soul. Don't follow a belief out of guilt or habit.

There are many paths to God. Wherever you are is perfect for your present awareness, or you wouldn't be there. You are always having the experiences in your life you need for your development, and this includes the religion or spiritual practice you are using now. Ultimately, for your own growth, you have to be willing to let go of any teaching that no longer serves you or helps you grow in your daily life. Remember, growth is living life as consciously as possible, on all levels: emotionally, mentally, physically, and spiritually. It is a commingling of Spirit that should have a powerful, positive, and practical impact on your daily life.

My Spiritual Evolution

My own spiritual evolution started out with Catholicism, which was perfect for my life when I came into this world. My parents were very devout Catholics. And if you know anything about that religion, you know there is an emphasis to stay in it or be damned to "hell." It's intimidating, to say the least.

As I searched, the Catholic Church's doctrines could no longer answer all my questions about life; neither did it help me feel connected to God. At fifteen, I left the Catholic Church. This was a major decision to follow my heart and do what I felt I needed for my own life. I didn't want to practice a religion just because my parents did. I had to experience truth for myself.

Then came the brief period in my life when I considered myself to be an atheist. I totally rejected God, the Holy Spirit, and all religion. I was on my own at the time, and it was a very dark period in my life. I kept observing life, though, and things I experienced and observed showed me there had to be some kind of larger intelligence in charge. I couldn't deny it. I felt there had to be a Source of all creation.

Then came my agnostic period. Agnostics believe there is a possibility of a God or higher intelligence, but they don't accept formalized religion. This period, which lasted two or three years, helped me have a little more peace, but I still felt a lack of con-nection to a Source, to Spirit. During this time I read a lot of self-help books, and I came across some very eye-opening spiritual teachings that talked about how in every moment each person creates the future by actions in the present. I had begun to believe in this spiritual principle myself, even before I read the books. The books just confirmed to me the truths I was observing.

During this time I tried learning how to meditate. The books suggested I sit still and make my mind blank, something I could never do. Either I got so still that I fell asleep, or I never reached the place of stillness that was supposed to connect you with God. Meditation was something I did infrequently at best. But I knew I needed to have a method to help me connect with Spirit consistently so I could raise my thoughts and energy above the negative hubbub, vibrations, and energy of the outer world.

About that time, along came Greg. We started to date when I was about twenty-five, and a year and a half later we got married. Our marriage was based in friendship and spiritual growth, and we are still good friends today. We divorced when we both realized we had grown as much as we could from our marriage, and we grew a lot from our knowing each other. We were both teacher and student, and he introduced me to an active spiritual practice, a sect of Buddhism. This sect of Buddhism taught about the effects and power of your thoughts and actions in your daily life, and that with each action you create your future. I found these teachings were in agreement with everything I'd come to know from my own observations.

I found Buddhism to be a spiritual practice I could stay awake with! It involved singing or chanting a high vibratory word. You chant this word every day for a period of time that feels comfortable for you. The act of using your voice in this manner helps raise your vibrations and change your energy toward the positive, toward your higher self.

So began my Buddhist period. It helped me tremendously. Through this next evolutionary step in my consciousness, I was able to stop being bulimic without therapy! This was a tremendous and powerful experience for me. I had been bulimic for fourteen years. Nothing else had stopped my urge to binge and purge, but raising my spiritual awareness and energy did! By using a high vibratory word every day my bulimia went away in just a few short months. My Buddhist practice taught me the value of a viable spiritual practice and the power of connecting daily to my higher self.

A spiritual practice, in my opinion, is a particular tool to reach your higher self and Spirit every day. It is not an isolated cry for help when things are rough; it is a tool you use with consistency and commitment for your advancement of consciousness and union with Spirit. It is similar to dedicated musicians or athletes who practice every day to become more skilled. If a spiritual practice is working for you, it will positively affect your daily life and help you have the courage to confront personal issues you may need to change in order to grow. There should be no separation from your spiritual awareness and your daily life.

I found I functioned only partially when I was not consistent with my spiritual practice. For me, it was like a car running on only two cylinders, or thinking you can have a perfect body without consistent good food and exercise. Buddhism taught me that to reach my goals, spiritual or otherwise, I had to be consistent with my actions. I learned that this consistency from beginning to end with thoughts, emotions, and physical movements achieves your desired results. You are either going forward or backward. There is no standing still!

Spiritual Practice and Prayer

There is a difference between a spiritual practice and typical prayer. Prayer can be a spiritual practice, or it can be a way to stay a victim. Most people pray by begging God or Spirit to help them out of some kind of unpleasant circumstance. When people pray as beggars, their energy in reality separates them from the Source of life. If you pray in this fashion, it is not a spiritual practice.

A spiritual practice is a tool to use every day, not just when you are feeling down. When you are using a spiritual practice, your goal is to become more connected to God and Spirit, so you can live your life from the energy of cause, which is a creative, active place. When you beg, even to God, you are a victim. Often people pray for years without realizing they are still taking actions that keep them powerless victims.

Any form of spiritual practice or prayer should empower your life if your inner intention is to be the master of your life, in union with Spirit. When you consciously take actions to produce what you want in your life, you live as the initiator, not the victim.

Changing My Spiritual Practice

Practicing Buddhism helped me feel and act positively and taught me that my actions do make a difference. This was a very empowering place to be. I was consistent with my spiritual practice every day, until I reached the inner knowing that it had taken me as far as it could. I felt I had learned all I could, and I wanted and needed a different spiritual practice. So as quickly as I accepted Buddhism, I left. That was a hard decision to make because of the social pressures from my years of practice with the other Buddhists who were my friends. But I knew in my heart I was ready for the next step in my spiritual development.

For several years I searched for my next spiritual step. I definitely wanted a spiritually active discipline. I learned from Buddhism that it is important for me to have a spiritual practice; otherwise, it's easy for me to get caught up in the mundane workings of life. By this time I knew if I kept asking from my heart for the right vehicle to appear that it would. It did, and it's called Eckankar, and I continue to practice it today.

Teachings As Soul

Eckankar teaches you how to contact the Holy Spirit or the Source of all life directly. Through the spiritual exercises in Eckankar, your consciousness is developed so you can awaken to *experience* yourself as Soul. The result is an increase in freedom, wisdom, and love in your life. Using the high vibratory words it teaches helps you to open your heart and life to Divine Love, which in the truest essence is God.

As my awareness expanded, I needed to let go of spiritual vehicles that no longer served me. If I feel the same way in the future about Eckankar, if I feel it is not fulfilling my needs, I will let it go as well. So far, I've never grown as fast or with as much joy and love as I have with this spiritual discipline.

None of my experiences with any spiritual path was wrong. At the time, each was perfect for my growth and the lessons I needed. It takes courage to leave the known for the unknown. It is easier to be complacent and stay in familiar thought patterns and experiences than to branch out and try something new. How many times have you tried something new that initially frightened you, but once you tried it you liked it and soon you became comfortable with it? A new way of thinking is no different.

Spiritual Unfoldment

As you grow in your spiritual life, things don't necessarily get easier. Sometimes things seem worse than they were before. Relax if you can, and know you ARE growing in the right direction whenever you focus on your spiritual development or on God.

As you bring more Spirit into your life, IT cleanses your negative karma and changes your vibrations from negative to positive. You are becoming a clear channel for Spirit. The more you take positive actions, the more you will create the positive in your life, even if at the moment you cannot see evidence of that fact.

In all your past lifetimes you incurred positive and negative karma. And as you open and grow in Spirit, your negative karma comes up for "restitution." It might be things you did yesterday, last month, or in another lifetime. But if you keep living from the conviction that the actions you take in the now do make a difference, eventually you will see the results of your positive efforts. Your awareness of life and how you live your life from this expanded consciousness is so much more rewarding. It is similar to your life as a baby — it was nice, but limited. As an adult you can appreciate life more, and you have more freedom than you did as a baby. So it is with spiritual development.

Clarifying the Confusion

Spiritual growth can get confusing because negative occurrences happen for various reasons. Perhaps you're focusing on things you don't want, causing energy or the vibration for them to come into your life through your physical actions or thoughts. Or it may seem that negative consequences happen because of positive spiritual actions. Actually positive actions are accelerating your growth, and causing the surfacing or burning off of old negative karma. Or, you may have hardships because Spirit is sending you a particular lesson. Maybe on the Soul level, unknown to your conscious self, you have asked to grow or learn a particular lesson. In order to evolve, Spirit might send you a particular experience to help you.

Sometimes it's hard not to get stuck in asking, "Why is this happening to me?" The best advice I can give you when you feel over-burdened is to get above the chattering of your mind by connecting to yourself as Soul. I do this by chanting different high vibratory words and spiritual visualizations. You may need to meditate, chant, or pray. Do something to rise above the energy of your emotions and mind. Remember, when things seem complicated and confusing, you are usually stuck in the workings of the conscious or unconscious mind. The mind always seems to make things confusing and complicated.

Soul, on the other hand, is simple. Soul is happy and peaceful; it is filled with joy. When things are balanced and peaceful and you are relaxed about what is happening, even if you would prefer it to be happening in a different way, then you are living more from the level of Soul.

Balancing Your Growth

In harder times, keep taking positive actions. Read something inspirational or do a Spiritual exercise, such as chanting a high vibratory word. You might even need to slow down on your Spiritual exercises. I know I tend to want growth now or, better yet, yesterday. Sometimes I get carried away and submerge myself with too many Spiritual exercises. Then negative karma surfaces, and sometimes it can be too much to handle. So I slow down for a day or two. Doing something very different and human, like going to a movie or exercising or just hanging out and being frivolous, sometimes helps balance out my growth and makes my life a little easier.

When your negative stuff surfaces, know you have the answers and solutions within you as Soul. Let yourself listen for the answers and be open to receive them. God and Spirit always are talking to you through other people, things you read, dreams you have, or the synchronistic occurrences you may easily overlook. If you are not in touch with your higher self, you may not hear the answers when Spirit is talking. Jesus Christ said, "Ask and you shall receive." The way to get any answer is to ask for it. It is always there to be had if you take responsibility to hear it, find it, and accept it.

You Are In Charge

You are in charge of your growth and its speed. Spirit gives you only what you can handle. Development of your true self can be fast or slow, depending on the actions you take with your heart, mind, and Soul. Changes don't necessarily occur because you are busy making all the "right" actions. Changes occur because you have voluntarily taken Spiritual truth into your consciousness.

To grow spiritually, you need complete freedom. In your outer world, you can be someone who is living the straight and narrow, but your spiritual growth may stop if you are making actions simply because someone said you should.

Let me give you an example. As a Catholic, I was told that to go to heaven or to become a more loving person, I had to go to mass every Sunday. For a while I did this faithfully and obeyed all the rules, but I felt I was getting nothing from these activities. If I had continued, I would have accomplished very little, because I wouldn't have been getting what I felt I needed for my own growth.

I want to emphasize this was my particular experience. If you are going to a church and following its precepts and feel filled with Spirit and it helps your life, keep with it. Each of us has to look within to find out what he or she needs to grow at any particular time.

Victim and Victor

Because I followed my free will in leaving the Catholic Church, I found out for myself what I needed in my life: how I needed to act, and what I needed to experience to unfold spiritually. We all are given that same free will. It is up to you to implement it. Until you use it, you will never be all you could be. You will remain a victim. Your happiness will always depend on what is happening in your environment, because you are not living from your power within. If something is taken away from you, then so goes your joy and peace of mind. That, to me, is not living freely.

Life is change. It is how you react to change that makes the difference in your life and whether you are truly free or bound by the outer picture of your life. Freedom and happiness come from within. Each moment, by your actions, you choose to be a victim or victor. What do you want from your life? The choice is yours. Remember, you are making that choice in each moment, right now!

CHAPTER 4

In Search of God

How do you describe
something that IS,
That is ALL,
seen and unseen,
felt and thought?

How do you describe
the unimaginable
and the imagined,
from the heart and mind
and Soul?

How do you describe
limitless light
and the purest of love,
emanating outward to all existence,
past, present, and future?

the only description then
. . . can be,
. . . GOD!

U nderstanding God from the intellectual, emotional, and physical parts of yourself are preliminary steps to prepare you to know God as Soul. So who or what is God? First, from my belief system, God is neither male nor female, just as Soul is neither male nor female. How will you know when you connect to God and your self as Soul? These are tough questions that I hope to clarify so you can have some intellectual and emotional awareness of what you may encounter when you grow as Soul. As you delve deeper, you will find some aspects of God are based in physical reality and some are from other levels and dimensions.

Knowing God and the Holy Spirit is an ongoing evolution, a never-ending process. Even after death, you continue to grow in your awareness of God and all that IT is. Let this chapter guide your further exploration of God and ITS many aspects.

Your understanding and realizations of God have to come from within yourself and your experiences. I share with you my present awareness — it is neither greater nor lesser than the awareness that lies within you. I hope sharing what I have come to know will speed your growth and understanding of God and Spirit and help you *concretely* in your daily life. I also hope it helps make knowing God a very real experience for you, not something you only grasp on an intellectual level. Keep in mind, your ability to experience a greater dimension of life comes from more than just your intellect.

The point of this book is help you learn to center your actions for your highest development and to develop a state of

indestructible happiness and awareness. How can you achieve
these without understanding and incorporating God into your
daily life? God and the Holy Spirit *are* life. You and I are the
individual, physical manifestations of THEM. When you learn
to connect directly to Spirit ("Spirit" and "Holy Spirit" here are
the same thing), your life will open up into new vistas. As you
work toward this direct connection, you have to develop, step
by step, on all levels in your awareness of God. Connecting
with God emotionally, mentally, and physically is paramount
to your lasting and real happiness. You need a preliminary
understanding of God before you can know and experience IT
directly as Soul.

Over the years, I have seen my clients change faster when
they incorporate Spiritual truths in their sessions and life. This
is because they work with their whole selves — their minds,
bodies, emotions, and spiritual selves.

Coming to know God and the workings of Spirit is an
incredibly personal journey. Someone can point the way for
you, but only you can travel your road. What you find on your
road reflects your consciousness at any particular time in your
life. Hopefully you can arrive at a state of consciousness where
you have a conscious knowing of God and Spirit from all parts
of your being.

God is perfect in all ways. The Divine is always here for
you; you just have to be able to comprehend and take in ITS
essence. If you limit your capacity for understanding, then
your experience of God will be limited. When your ability to
comprehend IT grows, so will your experience of God and
Spirit become greater and more all-encompassing.

This situation is similar to having an incredibly fine violin. This violin may be the most beautiful-sounding violin in
the world, but if your ability to play is on the beginner's

level, then the music you produce is vastly different than that of a master violinist. The violin, in itself, is perfect and has always been that way. What creates the different, beautiful sounds is the ability of the individual playing this violin. Moreover, hearing different people play the violin gives you new understandings of what is possible with this instrument. If you heard only people with mediocre talent play the beautiful violin, you might believe that was the only way it could sound. The same is true regarding my, or other people's, understandings of God and Spirit; it may broaden your capacity to understand and to be aware of new ways to approach your Spiritual journey when you are exposed to different ways of understanding God.

You have to make the effort to reach God and be open, just as the master violinist has made an effort to learn and practice. It takes more than just asking Spirit to come into your life for you to have this awareness. It takes action on all levels of your being. This principle is the same with anything you want to accomplish. You start out with desire, and follow through with consistent actions. Consistency of your actions from beginning to end with your body, mind, and emotions achieves results.

Let me give you an example. Let's say you want to lose weight. First you have desire, but just wishing to lose weight is not enough for you to accomplish your goal. You have to follow up that desire with consistent, appropriate actions, such as eating less, exercising, and handling the emotional problems that may have been a factor in gaining weight. The same thing is true with your spiritual development. It takes more than just asking for it or desiring it. It takes consistent action.

Aspects of God

Through my many encounters with different spiritual teachings and my own inner knowing, I feel it is important to understand the different aspects of God. Recognizing and understanding them helps you know where you are headed, and they can guide you on your journey. They are like a road map to your destination that makes your travel easier and faster.

First and foremost, God is Divine Love. This is what IT is. Emanating from God is Spirit, or what some religions call the Holy Spirit. Spirit is the energy that flows from God to the rest of creation, giving it life and form. Spirit is the heart of God. Spirit is the food for all of existence, seen and unseen, physical and spiritual.

Spirit is an extension of God that manifests as Sound, Light, and Divine Love. Sound, Light, and Divine Love are the forming "stuff' of all the universes, the forming and purifying power of life. When the Sound and Light of God purify you, you are more open for love, freedom, and wisdom to flow through your life. The Sound of God is the audible life-stream that uplifts you and helps you open your heart to all dimensions of love and to God. The Sound is similar to the vibrations created from the movement of molecules, but more so. When your inner awareness is attuned to the levels of God, you may be consciously aware of these vibrations or Sounds. The Light of God is the energy that makes up all of life.

You may already have heard the different Sounds of God and not realized it. The first time I remember hearing the Sound of God was when I was a child. My mom or dad would send me to bed and I would lay there terrified that a boogeyman would come out of my closet. As I lay in bed totally motionless with the covers over my head, I would hear this humming, similar to the sound of powerful electrical wires.

The Sound was comforting, but I didn't know what it was. Now when I hear sound, I realize it is Spirit's way of communicating to me, and it makes me more conscious of what is happening in the moment. Sound helps me gain more wisdom and clarity. If I had this knowledge of Sound when I was a child, I could have been more of an active participant by consciously allowing it to fill my being. Having knowledge gives you choices of how to use that knowledge. The more you are aware of how life works, the more fully and consciously you can participate in your life.

Knowing there may be many worlds of existence and many ways to experience reality may help you to participate more fully should you encounter Sound and Light or different universes in your dreams or contemplations. These universes are where Souls live, grow, and learn. They have their own qualities and governing laws.

When I speak of the worlds of existence, I describe them in a general way, because everyone has a personal experience of a place. It is like describing a city you have visited to a friend who hasn't been there. You might speak in general terms about your experience of that place. When your friend visits there at another time, the experiences might be different, and your friend's description might differ from yours. Neither one of you is wrong in your observations: both of you have been there but you just have had different experiences of the same place.

Simply look around this planet and see all the different cultures. This planet is a miniscule part of a whole physical universe. It would be nearly impossible for one person to fully describe fully all the aspects of life on this physical planet, or any of the other universes, because of the limitations of an individual's viewpoint and the enormity of the places involved.

Physical Universe

First there is the physical universe. This is where you are now. The physical universe has laws of gravity and cause and effect, and material properties that include energy, space, and time. It is the most dense of all the universes.

The term dense refers to how Light and Sound form physical creations. An example of this is that ice is denser than steam — the energy that makes up steam is less dense than its counterpart of ice. The difference between the two creations is how dense or solid the molecules of energy are. (Remember this analogy as I describe the other universes.)

Any world of form of any kind is called a "lower" world, because it is less than pure Spirit. In these worlds you still need some kind of body for Soul to use so it can function in that particular vibration. (Vibrations, once again, are the movement of the Light and Sound. Vibrations are simply energy. Any kind of body is made up of energy.)

On the physical level of existence, there is less Light and Sound apparent. Compared to the others, the life lessons of the physical universe are harder, but because of these life lessons, you have more opportunities to change your negative karma. The classical spiritual Sound associated with this plane is thunder, though your spiritual self can hear other Sounds. This is the world of the senses. The color most associated with this plane is green.

Astral Universe

The next highest world is the astral. This universe has more Light, Sound, and freedom. It is bigger than the physical universe and the laws that govern it are different. The inhabitants of the astral universe can look like us, but their bodies are less dense and have more Spiritual light. Their vibrations of energy are finer, and they can move about freely by just thinking. This is the plane of emotion, the highest place most people reach by astral projection. The Sound associated with this world is the roar of the sea, and its predominant color is pink.

Causal, Mental, and Etheric Universes

The next worlds, in succession, are the Causal, Mental, and Etheric. When I use the words "higher" or "lower" in describing these worlds, understand they are linear descriptions. In this world of space and time, we think in terms of "up" and "down," "higher" and "lower." In truth, these different worlds exist simultaneously. You experience them when your consciousness is of a similar vibration. You can experience them even in this physical plane through your dreams or contemplations. I believe my dreams are real experiences, so when I dream or I am in contemplation and I see or hear the aspects of these different universes, I actively use this information to help me through problems here. For example, if I saw a pink color through a contemplation, that might be an indicator that something is bothering me or an emotional issue needs attention. (Pink, remember, is the color of the astral plane and it corresponds with emotions.) Soul is always communicating with your human consciousness in ways you can understand. Becoming more conscious of your signposts helps you to unblock obstacles to your direct knowing of God and Spirit.

These next levels are also mixtures of Spirit and in some kind of form. The color designated for the Causal world is orange and the Sound there is the tinkling of bells. The Mental plane is blue and the Sound is running water. The Etheric, which is the highest world with some kind of form, has the predominant color purple and the Sound of buzzing bees. All the worlds can have all colors and all Sounds.

The upper worlds are larger and more spiritual, and they have less form and more Spirit. There is still some kind of body covering Soul, but the bodies are less dense and are made up of finer molecules. Each body has a unique vibrational rate, as we do here on Earth. In the higher worlds, the bodies get finer and finer and are more light-filled. They are closer to being pure Spirit.

Duality or Polarity

Duality or polarity is the way you learn in the lower worlds of God. Duality means something composed of contrary or opposite qualities. Let's take an example of duality that is found on Earth. To experience warmth, you must experience cold. To experience a positive, there must be a negative. To have a mountain, there must be a valley. The intrinsic nature of form is duality. When there is form, you cannot escape having opposites.

Having some kind of body indicates some form of duality, and duality is something less than the pure Soul experience. Your ultimate goal should be to evolve to the pure spiritual state. Since you have a body and you are here now, you need to work toward your ultimate goal with great care and respect for your human life. Ending your life sooner than your natural lifespan is a negative action, and you would have to return to face the karma you incurred. A necessary step in your evolution as Soul is being human and encountering and growing through your lessons. You can never escape the lessons or karma you need to have in order to be your truest self.

In the higher realms of God, in all the worlds "higher" than the Etheric, there is no form, and so, no duality. You reside as pure Spirit: Light, Sound, and Divine Love. You no longer need a body. You are one with the Light and Sound of

God, one with Spirit and Divine Love. The upper worlds are the pure worlds of Light, Sound, Divine Love, being, and knowing. They are impossible to describe with words, because words are of the lower universes. Words come from the mind, and Soul is above the mind.

In these worlds, you are no longer encumbered with karma. You have complete freedom. You take on and experience karma only when you are in the lower worlds. The worlds above the physical universe are what the Bible calls heaven. Heaven is not a place where people mill about in flowing robes having a good time; the Heavens are active states that are always changing and growing, just like on Earth. As Soul, you are always changing, learning, and growing because God cannot be fully known.

God and Your Daily Life

Consequently how does knowing God pertain to your daily life here and your potential happiness? If you don't have a goal or a destination in mind, then getting ahead or being in control of your life is greatly diminished (or blocked altogether).

Knowing your goal gives you purpose and direction. You can ascertain what actions to take here and know how to reach your destination only when you know what it is. We all want happiness. Most of us want peace, security, and joy, but most people I see in my sessions and regular people in the world today are unconscious about what life and living is all about.

Most people on this planet are less than satisfied with their lives. Many feel powerless, and they don't know what to do to achieve deeper satisfaction and peace.

If you live only from the small consciousness of your mind, ego, and emotions, you will never experience the true greatness life has to offer. It is only when you get beyond the human state of consciousness that anything lasting comes into your life. The reality on Earth is that all things change. The only constant is change. So if you consistently put your energy into things of limited duration, no true joy can stay in your life. Think about it: If you don't know the rules of life, how can you participate fully? When you dedicate your life to the limitless reality of Spirit and God, true meaning and happiness can be yours now, in this lifetime.

Let's put this idea to work. Most of us work, pay our bills, get married, have children, cry, laugh, overcome hardships, eat, sleep, and have fun. This doesn't change. It is not what you do that counts so much as where you focus your awareness and attention *while* you make these actions. Your focus creates your connection to God and develops your inner growth. Aspire to make your life actions in the name of God, not just for your human ego or for physical survival. When you come from this point of Spirit, you live each day eliminating negative karma, and your chances of creating new negative karma are greatly reduced. Your daily life becomes something very special indeed!

You create negative karma when you make actions based solely from your lower self, like the ego or bodily desires. That's not to say actions from your ego or physical self can't be positive, but generally when you come from your lower self, your actions are usually self-centered. You might not consider the whole of life, so the possibility of producing negative karma is greater when you come from the ego.

When you start the day dedicating your daily actions to God, you raise your vibrations and work with God's will. When you dedicate your actions to Spirit, you allow Spirit to flow through you, positively affecting your daily life and your actions. You positively affect everything and everyone around you, whether you or anyone else is aware of it or not.

We are all part of God, so there is no separation between you and all of life. When you live from an enlightened awareness, you know all creatures are a part of God and thus, a part of you. Whatever you do to create value for yourself creates value for the whole of life, and whatever you do to create value for others *without devaluing yourself* is also good for you.

Living from this higher state does not mean losing yourself in any way. It is NOT being a martyr. What it does mean is living in an individual way without impinging on others. It means living the happiest, most fulfilled life you can, while staying in harmony and purpose with God and Spirit by being your authentic self. This is accomplished through your daily actions. Your actions and energy become teachers for others, to help them know what life is about.

Martyrdom

I was taught, as many of us were, that to be a good person meant you had to be a martyr. You did not allow yourself to love yourself fully. Everyone else's desires took precedence over your own. Being a martyr means sacrificing self-esteem or desire, even to the point of hurting your own health or well-being. Martyrs, in my opinion, are victims!

I wanted very much to be a loving and evolved person. So I let people walk all over me because I thought this was what being "loving" meant — negating the self. I ended up stuffing a lot of anger, and I didn't love myself. For years I had terribly low self-esteem, and I didn't allow myself to live in a healthy way. I became a victim under the guise of wanting to be a good person.

Think now, how can you love anyone, including God, if you don't love yourself? How can you let love into your being if you are a victim? This is what I came to terms with. I began to realize that being truly happy and loving God and all ITS creatures begins with self-love and self-respect.

Love Yourself

Spirit does not ask you to deny yourself for others or to be a martyr. The Holy Spirit asks that you be all you can be and allow IT to move through you to affect others in a non-invasive, non-controlling way. Only when you love yourself and you do what is best for your life can you be a healthy vehicle for Spirit. Only then can you truly love others fully. You accomplish this when you first give yourself love and self-respect.

One way to love yourself (You are part of the whole of life that you need to love. So when you love yourself you love God.) is by establishing your personal growth process and boundaries. You are the one who has to meet your needs and defend yourself when people try to control you. You are in charge of your life! Each individual is unique, so the requirements for your life are different than anyone else's.

Only when you love yourself can you truly know Spirit. Loving yourself sometimes means saying no to others' requests. The more you give yourself what you need and base your actions on becoming a more aware and loving person, the more you will become connected to God. Spirit will then flow through you in a natural way to bring Light, Sound, and Divine Love to you and others around you. This is true service.

Spiritual service, unlike martyrdom, is a blend of self-love and nurturing that allows Spirit to flow through you while you do what you need to do for your happiness and growth. Service is not giving up things you like to do. Service is an attitude, an intention, a state of being you have while you do the things you love to do in your life.

Observe the victims and martyrs you know. Do they bring light and love to anyone? Think of all the bright, happy, self-fulfilled people you know. Aren't they truly doing God's work by being happy? The energy of victims and martyrs is negative, constrictive, and dark; the energy of a self-loving person is expansive, lighter, and brighter. When people who love themselves declare themselves to be vehicles for God, all their actions take on a greater effectiveness because they send Light and Divine Love to others as Soul. Sometimes, by their presence, others are brought closer to God. What counts in spiritual growth is the consciousness of the individual, how close and connected one is to Spirit in daily life.

Treating yourself with love and respect is your first link with God. You then can affect other people without interfering with their free will. This is an important point! Linking up with Spirit and God does not entail forcing or controlling others to think or be any certain way. Think of yourself as an open tube. Allow the Light and Sound of God to flow through you, while being detached to the effect it may have on others. Be unconcerned about whether others are open to receive Spirit because you know it is not up to you to control others' growth.

Contemplation, Meditation or Prayer

So how do you bring Spirit and God into your life? You can do this by a process called contemplation, which brings Divine Love, Light, and Sound of Spirit and God into every part of yourself. Contemplation is not like prayer or meditation, which are more passive ways to connect with God. Contemplation is active. In contemplation, you are actively uniting with Spirit. You are not passively waiting for IT to come to you.

A client in a seminar I was conducting described beautifully the difference between the three practices. She said prayer is the vehicle one uses to talk to God, meditation is when you are listening to God and contemplation is your union with God, Spirit, or yourself as Soul.

When you go above your emotions and your mind as Soul in contemplations, changes in your life occur faster and they are more comprehensive than with meditation or prayer. With contemplation, you link up with yourself as Soul — you actively seek out higher awareness.

Soul is the life force of being human. Consequently when you contact Soul in your daily life, as with contemplations, it affects all parts of you in a most positive way. We each have parts that make us human: Soul, the conscious and unconscious mind, the emotional self, and the physical self. These are real bodies within your physical body. When Soul leaves, your physical body dies. The growth and connection you make with Spirit and Soul during contemplation has an effect on your physical life now and after death. This is the greatest growth you can have. Contemplation is a very powerful tool for anyone to use to connect with Spirit or God.

Contemplation brings you into union with Divine Love and the twin aspects of Sound and Light. It helps open your heart to all levels of love. (I'm emphasizing the aspects of Sound and Light here because I have devoted a whole chapter to the subject of love.)

Sound and Light are the basic purifying elements of God and Spirit. There are Sound and Light on every plane of existence, and the purely Spiritual planes are filled only with Sound and Light. The closer you get to God, the brighter the Light and the more beautiful the Sound.

Light on Earth is experienced most commonly through spiritual practices. It is seen by your inner vision, which sometimes is called your "third eye." It is a tool for Soul to see Light and hear Sound while in the physical body. Know, as your awareness grows, you may hear Sound and see Light outside of your formal contemplations. The more you expand your awareness through contemplation, the more you will connect and unify with Sound and Light. These aspects of God help cleanse you of negativity and open you to Spirit. The changes usually start at the level of Soul and filter to the rest of you.

The Light of Spirit can come in all colors. Sometimes the Light of Spirit is seen as stars, specks that sparkle, flashes, or larger pointed stars. Many times the stars are blue. It doesn't matter what form or color the Light takes, just know the Light is of Spirit. If and when you see Light, it is a sign your consciousness is being uplifted for a deeper understanding of life and helping you know on some level what you need in order to grow. You see Light and hear Sound according to the levels of your consciousness. As you grow in awareness, your ability to hear different Sounds of Spirit and see the different Light grows.

Of the two aspects of God, Sound — the movement or speed of the vibrations of energy on any certain level of existence — is the more important. Sound is important because it helps balance spiritual growth in your physical body. Sound is an indication you are making changes, and it has many diverse functions. One function of Sound is pure God energy moving through you, rearranging aspects of your being that are not in alignment with Spirit.

Also if you grow too fast in spiritual consciousness, you may feel unbalanced emotionally, mentally, or physically. One property of Sound is to help you balance your whole self while you grow and change. Sound monitors your growth.

The numerous Sounds you can hear in contemplation are like those on the physical plane: thunder, wind, bells, a single note of the flute, violins, and humming like that of electrical wires, to name just a few. You will know they are spiritual when you hear them unconnected to what would normally cause them. For example, if you hear thunder when there is no storm in sight or hear the buzzing of bees when you know there are none around, you can assume you have heard Sound.

Sound is God's way of communicating to you. The Sound of God has always been. Sound is even mentioned in the Bible when the apostles heard the rushing of the wind at the Last Supper and when, "In the beginning there was the Word." Few religions teach about Sound, or if they do, most do not know how to contact it. This is why it is fundamental to have a daily spiritual practice, to be connected again to your true roots. Contemplations help you connect to the Sound and Light of God!

Exercise

Choosing a High Vibratory Word

An extremely powerful way to start your contemplation is to sing or chant the oldest name for God, HU. HU (pronounced like the name Hugh or the color designation hue) raises your vibrations. When you elevate your vibrations, you go above your mind and emotions and connect directly with the Holy Spirit and to a higher state of awareness. It is analogous to climbing to higher ground to find your way if you are lost. Your perspective from the higher ground is broader and more accurate. This is what you do when you chant any high vibratory word. You set up your energy to accept and understand Spirit and God from a higher perspective.

Some other high vibratory words are God, Aum, Wah Z, Divine Love, or Sugmad, which is another name for God. Choose one that feels right for you.

Then close your eyes, sit comfortably with your feet flat on the floor, and focus gently on the place between your eyes. As you exhale, sing your word of choice. Elongate the word as you exhale. (HU will sound like HUUUUUUU and Wah Z will sound like Waaaahhhh Zeeeeeee, and so forth.)

Do this for ten to twenty minutes. You may see a blue light or hear some of the Sounds I've mentioned. Whatever happens, know you are linking up as Soul with Spirit and that you are safe and protected. Sometimes it may seem like nothing is happening, but the very use of the word HU (or any of the other words) will raise your vibrations and bring you spiritual protection and growth in every aspect of your life. This is especially true when you consistently incorporate contemplations in your daily routine. ⌣

Prepare with Feeling

After you have sung your word for ten to twenty minutes, use your imagination to increase your connection with Spirit. Your imagination is a powerful tool to help you grow as Soul. If you can't clearly visualize, that's okay. The more you do it, the better you get. The key is to relax and let go of mental expectations of what is supposed to happen. Just doing the process helps you grow and whatever happens is what you need.

It is very important to begin any contemplation with a feeling of love. Love is the golden key to changing yourself and bringing you closer to knowing God in this lifetime. If love is hard for you to bring up or feel, try to remember a time when you were in love or felt love for a pet or a friend. The more you fill your heart with love during your contemplation, the more love comes into your daily life. Love connects you with God, for God is love. ⌣

Connecting to Spirit and God is experiential. As with anything else, the more you practice, the better you get. Therefore,
if you have never tried a spiritual contemplation, give yourself
lots of time and acceptance. Experiment honestly with it for a
period of time, a month or two, and then compare how you feel
and how you experience life after that time. Remember you are
in charge of your life. You have the freedom to create your contemplations any way you want so they are pertinent to you. Your
imagination is a function of the higher part of you. It is a powerful aspect to creating. Before anything becomes physically manifested in this reality it starts with the imagination. For example,
an architect imagines a house before drawing the plans. What
comes first is always the imagination.

The next exercises include suggestions for what to do after
you've sung your chosen word for a few minutes. Feel free to use
these visualizations, or create your own.

Your Inner Child

*This exercise has helped me work with my inner
child (the name I give my emotional self) and
helped me work through negative feelings about
myself. Most of us have a wounded emotional self,
which is stuck in childhood. I've imagined my adult
self re-educating my inner child to help her love herself more and help her overcome fears that were
brought on by living in a dysfunctional family.
Here's how: Pick different scenarios in your past
where you once felt unsafe, shamed, unloved, or
angry. Let your adult self connect emotionally with
your inner child. If your inner child has been
unloved, change the past situation so your inner
child feels love unconditionally. If your father or
mother abused you, give your inner child a chance
to safely express anger and then give it new, loving,
understanding role models.*

Remember this is a process, and as you heal one aspect of your inner child, you strengthen yourself to feel and heal more issues. It doesn't matter what the problems are now or where the problems began. Always remember the power to change anything in your life is in the present and endless now. ∽

Spiritual School

Another visualization is to see yourself in a higher world of beautiful light. Imagine yourself learning life, love, and wisdom at Spiritual schools, taught by Spiritual masters. Use all your senses. Hear words of wisdom, feel love, see yourself getting the answers to your questions or problems. Your imagination is real and creates. When you are in contemplation and imagining, what you imagine really happens on some level in your being. ∽

Receiving Divine Help

During another contemplation, after you have sung your word, visualize yourself standing in a beautiful river of light. See a spiritually loving being like Christ, Buddha, or a Guardian Angel next to you. See yourself giving that loving being all your anger, fears, questions, worries, or anything else you want to let go of. Try to feel and receive the love that emanates from this being and know you are being helped. See the being accepting what you gave, putting it in a basket, and letting it float down the river of Light. Feel yourself cleansed and filled with Divine Love, Light and the Sound of God. ∽

Spiritual Travel

Another exercise to try, after you have sung your chosen word, is to imagine yourself leaving your physical body. See yourself standing outside your physical body and looking at it. Imagine white light around your physical body and know you are safe. Look around the room.

Now ask for only a divine, loving being to help you grow spiritually, to appear. At this time you may want to chant Wah Z. Wah Z is a Spiritual traveler that helps you as Soul to stretch spiritually and keeps you completely safe. You can ask these guides any questions or you can be open to receive love and suggestions for further growth. Try to see both yourself and the loving being as sparkles of light, like thousands of little stars. ᔐ

Contemplations can be limitless! The key to reaching the highest states of being is to do them daily with love. State before you start your day that your actions are a vehicle for Spirit and God. With that, your life will evolve in love and higher awareness. You will realize why you are here. Everything in your life, your every action, takes on the qualities of mercy and love. You then become the messenger of God, even while you sleep.

Dreams

As you grow in Spirit, you also grow in awareness of the realities you can experience. Your dreams might become more lucid. You may feel like you are experiencing the things depicted in your dreams, and they may seem clearer. Dreams are a very real part of your life, a way for Spirit to communicate to you. Some dreams are from a purely to-teach-you basis, where Soul is getting information for its growth. Other dreams are prophetic. Sometimes you may learn things in your dreams that help your daily life go a little smoother. Others are true Soul journeys out of the body to other inner worlds you will remember as dreams. As you focus on your dreams, you will begin to know what they are trying to convey to you. Keeping a dream journal helps you focus on your dreams and helps you remember them. As you grow toward God, your consciousness is awakened both in the day and night with your dreams. When this happens, you can use every moment to grow and learn.

Waking Dreams

Spirit talks to you in the daytime by waking dreams or the synchronicity of events. The more you are tuned to Spirit, the more you understand the message. Let me give you some examples of waking dreams.

For years I have tried to overcome my fear of being alone and vulnerable. Being on my own at fifteen left a lot of pain and hurt in my life and an underlying belief I was alone in life without protection. This affected almost every aspect of my life. I found it very hard to feel secure and safe. Little snags that come up in my daily life can appear as very real threats to my security. Let me give you an example.

One day my car battery died unexpectedly. Then the very same day I got a speeding ticket. The next week, my car had a flat tire at night. I left it in the shop all the next day so the tire could be repaired, and I told them to lock it and leave it in their parking lot so I could pick it up after I finished working. After I saw my last client, I got a ride to the garage and I discovered my car was locked in for the night!

These occurrences were a waking dream for me. I felt a spiritual message in the situations since they all occurred close together. In all those situations, someone was right there to help me. Even with the flat tire, a motorist called the police (this was before cell phones), and one came within five minutes. This particularly had an impact on me because in the past I had felt so alone and afraid, and without transportation, I felt particularly vulnerable. The Spirit was telling me I was protected.

During each situation I silently chanted HU to myself and acted to remedy the situation as best I could. There was always a ride, and I never lost any work. I now have a deeper trust in the protection of Spirit, and I know trust is necessary for my further growth as Soul. What seemed like annoyances were really Spirit giving me valuable lessons and support.

This is one example of a waking dream. Another happened when a friend I respect encouraged me to go into a business deal with him. The business was a training company that dealt with self-growth. I had never heard of the company before my friend mentioned it. The investment was affordable but a stretch financially. Inwardly I kept asking Spirit what I should do, to give me a sign for my highest good. The next day during a session a client mentioned this company and the really bad experience she had with them. After the session I was even more confused. I respected my friend and his opinion, yet my client had reported a negative experience. I kept doing my spiritual exercises and continued to ask for guidance. Two days later a new client started talking about his background, and again this company came up. His experience was also bad. Well, I am a slow learner. I weighed both clients' experience and the enthusiasm of my friend and was still undecided. I did nothing and still asked for Spiritual guidance. The very next day another client, during her session, spoke about this company and her negative experiences. She was quite vehement and angry toward the company.

Well, there is a powerful element regarding the number three. Three times in one week, three different clients — without my asking — related their bad experiences about this company. I finally got the message. (Sometimes I need the proverbial Spiritual two-by-four to hit me over the head. This was one of those times.)

I called my very enthused friend and told him I decided not to invest in this venture with him. Because of the deep respect I had for him (and still do) I still felt I might be missing out on a great financial deal, but the three unsolicited, angry testimonials from my clients convinced me to opt out.

About six months later I ran across my friend at an art fair. During our conversation I asked him how he did with the business deal. He got very quiet and then he said that he went bankrupt. He told me that the leadership of the company was unethical. I felt badly for him but very fortunate that I had listened to my waking dream.

Waking dreams can be as simple as several people telling you to go to a certain doctor when you have been asking Spirit for guidance about your health. Spirit is always talking to you — through other people, nature, books and road signs. The ways in which Spirit can communicate with you are limitless! For example, you can ask a question, pick up a spiritual book, randomly pick a page, and see what phrase hits you.

Waking dreams are around you all the time. You just have to be aware enough to watch, look and listen for the communication. The more aware you are, the more you notice Spirit speaking to you through your daily life, helping you to learn and grow.

In finding God, you have free will. You can be the victim and wait for Spirit to contact you, or you can take an active role in reaching God. I believe taking an active role is the only way anyone reaches God and God's love, in life or death. Know when you desire to connect with Spirit IT is always here for you when you are ready!

CHAPTER FIVE

Relationships

The robin calls
to his mate,
his song is one only she
can relate.

Their dance begins
again...
song to song
flight entwined.

Soaring ever higher
yet at times just perched,
overlooking the world
together — yet apart.

Sharing is their dance
their flight of life,
one encouraging the other
to the endless reaches
of their possibilities.

R elationships can run the gamut from painful to bliss-
ful, and they can create a great deal of confusion. If
you try to escape having relationships, you still have
to deal with yourself. In this chapter, I'll simplify the confusion
that comes from relating to others, yourself, and life, and I'll discuss the more day-to-day workings of being human.

Your Relationship with Yourself

The most important relationship in your life is the one
you have with yourself. Until you are clear about your relationship with yourself no other relationship in your life will be
clear. Consequently, you won't know how to relate to others
in worthwhile ways.

Always keep in mind that your true essence is Soul, and
all relationships in life are actually tools to help bring you to
this understanding and awareness. Attaining unconditional
love and understanding yourself are vital requirements to this
awareness. Many people have no idea what will make them
happy. Often, they search for identity and happiness through
experiences, through other people, or by acquiring things.
Many people never really know themselves. Knowing yourself
and knowing your needs as an individual are crucial to your
day-to-day and overall happiness. This is true whether your
desire is a higher awareness of yourself as Soul or not.

You will never find true happiness outside yourself! If
that sounds like a strong statement to you…good. You are the
only one who can make you happy, and the faster you come to

this realization the quicker you can have the happiness you seek. It's imperative for you to fulfill your own needs as an individual to make this happen. You do this by letting yourself know what you need, then by giving yourself those things that are essential for your happiness.

A Healthy Self

There are many opinions about what constitutes a healthy self. My definition of a healthy self is someone who consistently makes loving actions with his or her life. A healthy self is someone who loves himself or herself just for being, not for what he or she does or has accomplished. Healthy people allow their needs to be met on every level — spiritual, mental, emotional, and physical.

Healthy individuals know only they can make their lives happy. Being a healthy person means treating yourself as you would treat another person when you are deeply in love. It's respecting yourself enough to say "no" when you really want to say "no" and not feel guilty. It's realizing other people's feelings are not more important than yours.

These are just some fundamental aspects to a healthy relationship with your self. Basically, no one can change anything in your life for you but you.

Unhealthily Relating

Let's look at some components of relating in unhealthy ways. People who compensate for their bad feelings about themselves consciously or unconsciously can mask these feelings by seeking approval and worth through other people, things, or accomplishments. They try to get love and approval outside of themselves. This may manifest by their becoming either super-responsible nurturers or martyrs. Both are victims. They basically let themselves be abused, and the abuse they allow into their lives can be emotional, mental, or physical. They believe (consciously or unconsciously) they are powerless to change the circumstances in their life, and they do not allow their needs to be met. They sabotage their control and personal power in their life. I tell my clients there are really only two kinds of people: victims and people who give themselves permission to use their personal power to create what they want in life to be healthy and truly joyful.

Unhealthy people may be making choices in response to a negative inner image. If this is true for you, that inner belief is coloring everything in your life. Until you change that negative inner belief, you may try to compensate for your negative feelings about yourself by living as a martyr or a dysfunctional nurturer.

Dysfunctional Nurturer

The super nurturers, the overly responsible people, are trying unconsciously to get love and to feel whole. Unconsciously they feel if they do for others, then they are good people and they can love themselves. They tend to overstep other people's boundaries, trying to control others by making choices for them, manipulating, or overextending themselves in other people's lives. They do much more for others than is healthy, and they usually cover up their own feelings to protect others. A typical belief or response of a dysfunctional nurturer would be to withhold opinions or suppress anger because "it would hurt the other person too much if I told them I was angry," or "if they truly knew how I felt they just couldn't take it."

Dysfunctional nurturers take responsibility for other people's feelings, responses, and actions. In doing so, they negate themselves. This is not living honestly or healthily. Withholding necessary communication and feelings or trying to second-guess and protect others from their feelings does not create honest self-growth, self-worth or healthy relationships.

More . . . Martyr

Martyrs, on the other hand, do not take responsibility for their lives. They blame the environment, circumstances, or other people for their lack of a happy life. These people usually have a hard time standing up for themselves and they allow others to step all over them. Martyrs hardly ever allow themselves to do what they truly want to do. They "sacrifice" their happiness and needs for others even when it is detrimental to their overall well-being and happiness.

You can even play both roles. Either way, your relationship with yourself or others is one of degradation, and degradation is not the way to get the inner love and peace you so dearly want. If your inner martyr or dysfunctional nurturer is letting you be abused, by your own actions or by the actions of others, you are not uplifting or loving yourself or the other person. This is definitely not the way to a healthy self or healthy relationships.

Remember, even if you didn't know it at the time, you created this role, so you have the power to change it. To change your role in life, you must realize how you are living your life. This realization is your first step toward a truly healthy relationship with yourself.

Unconditional Love

You need to love yourself unconditionally! Understanding this is imperative for your general happiness and higher ways of being. It is that simple and that profound!

Too many of us have grown up with the belief that in order to be good, we have to deny our own needs. This simply is not true. People have the spiritual right to be an individual and to do what is best for their life. My life is different than yours, and your life is different from anyone else's. Since our lessons are different, our needs are different. Remembering this is crucial to your health and happiness. If you are causing no harm to others and not interfering with or trying to control other people's lives or space, doing whatever you need to do for your happiness is not only correct, but also necessary and vital for your personal and spiritual growth.

To attain unconditional love, happiness, and spiritual advancement, inner shame from your childhood or other traumas in your life needs to be healed. You need to understand deeply that you are worthwhile as a person, just for being part of God. Fully understanding how you have been living is crucial to changing the old patterns that are preventing you from creating the life you want. When you understand this, you will probably have to learn new, healthier ways of living.

For example, if you tend to want to "fix" people, understand that other people have lessons to learn and the right to fix themselves or not. If you tend to live as a victim, you have to realize it is up to you to take charge of your life before you can be happy.

Healing Yourself First

True happiness and self-love can only be achieved when you heal your self. Look inside. Take a long hard look at your actions. See if you try to be more complete through relating and doing for others while neglecting yourself. Do you try to do this or that for someone so the other person will love you? Do you consistently seek approval to feel worthwhile? Do you tend to feel and act on the inner belief that other people's feelings and needs are more important than your own? Your self-worth may be more fragile than you think if you need a great deal of outside approval. Some people find themselves doing almost anything (often unconsciously) for outward approval because they have not learned to validate themselves. With inner validation comes freedom.

When you live with the belief that others are more valuable than you, or if you lose your individuality and self in order to get love and approval, then you deny yourself love and respect. All your relationships, including the one with yourself, get out of balance, and you lose love or never attain the love you so fervently seek.

Let me give you an example. Because I came from a dysfunctional family, my opinions and deep feelings of myself were ones of shame. Inside I felt worthless. I did not give myself permission to be treated with respect, nor did I give myself many words of praise or love. Because I did not approve of myself, my self-talk was very negative and critical most of the time. When I was on my own for the first couple of years, my bad feelings about myself peaked. I allowed myself to be abused physically by men, and financially I was just making it. I didn't feel good enough about myself to stop others from overstepping my boundaries. Because I didn't love or respect myself, how could others? I constantly felt I didn't count and that my feelings were unimportant or less important than other people's. I was trying to get love and self-worth by being a doormat and a victim. I so desperately wanted love that I lost my individuality and self-respect though I was totally unconscious of this at the time.

I remember one particular relationship when I was in my early twenties. The man in my life was verbally, emotionally, and physically abusive. There was nothing positive in this relationship — he was even mean to my cat! I stayed with him though I got nothing but negativity. I felt I had no choice. I wanted love. But was this love? I know now it wasn't. At that time in my life, desperate for approval and love and empty inside, I allowed myself to be treated badly.

I remember something clicked inside me one night when I was coming home from work. I realized I was allowing this abuse to happen. It wasn't so much that he was abusing me as it was that I was giving my permission to be abused. With this realization, I felt liberated. From that night on I took steps to free myself from abuse, and I left him.

This is a lesson I have never forgotten. I attracted that abusive man into my life because I hated myself, so I only had myself to blame. I once again made myself a victim and created my own hell! Unconsciously I thought if I did enough for others or for him, then I'd be worthy of love. I had it backwards. Now I know that if I raise up myself and truly love all parts of myself, I attract all the respect, goodness, and love I deserve.

The analogy I give my clients is this: If you are starving and have been eating moldy food to survive, you won't want to give it up. That moldy food has been keeping you alive, though just barely. When you learn to love and respect yourself it is like eating from a glorious buffet, and then you thrive! You deserve the glorious buffet — limitless supplies of love, and all that is positive.

To create and keep love and positive things in your life, it is necessary to know how your inner beliefs draw corresponding experiences to you.

Like Attracts Like

Your body is composed of cells and atoms. Scientists know there are even smaller particles than these, and all particles of energy vibrate. You are energy vibrating at a certain rate. Your thoughts, emotions, and actions influence and create your vibrational rate. In reality you are just vibrating energy! Your thoughts and feelings are also energy. This energy comes in a myriad of forms and densities. Like attracts like. You attract circumstances and relationships to you on the basis of your vibrational rate.

Physical objects, emotions, and thoughts vibrate at different rates. Though it seems like there is a separation between the physical, emotional, and mental parts of life, in reality all are ever-moving energy. What makes them appear separate is that everything vibrates at different rates of speed, creating different densities, such as gases and solids, thoughts and emotions.

All energy, all of us, is part of Spirit. Spirit makes up all of what you think of as reality. Different things, such as plants, animals, and humans, have different consciousness or awareness of life, and they also have different rates of vibration.

Your vibrational rate is your magnet. Your essence or being is vibrating energy and thus attracts, or "magnetizes," situations to you that reflect the total you. So if your total being vibrates with worthlessness, then you will attract or "magnetize" people and circumstances that reflect those vibrations. It is the same with self-love.

In my past, I believed men were not there for me or would treat me unkindly. I came to this belief because of my relationships with my brothers and my father. When I started to date, I attracted self-centered, uncaring, and, in some cases, abusive men. I was vibrating from the state of worthlessness. When I started to change my relationship with myself, I saw that the men I attracted were kinder and nicer. Changing the relationship with myself changed my vibrational rate; consequently, changing the situations and people I attracted into my life.

Changing Your Outer Environment

Your relationship with yourself is the key to changing your relationships with everyone else in your life. Other people in your life are mirrors, reflecting back to you what you need to change in your life. Your interactions with other people also tell you what you need to change within your own self. For example, if your co-workers or family victimizes you, try looking inside yourself to see what you need to change. If someone treats you in a way that you don't like, examine your relationship with yourself. If you have been attracting abuse, change within yourself the beliefs or emotional issues that created this in your life. When you do this, you will find that either the abusive person or persons will treat you better, they will leave your life, or you will leave theirs.

When you change, your environment has to change. This change in your environment has to happen because as you change your consciousness — you change your vibrations. Changing your consciousness changes your level of awareness or how "awake" you are living your life. As you may have already gathered, life can be lived in a limited, fundamental, survival mode, or with the realization that you are a spiritual being with a definite purpose for living.

Your outer environment, including the people in your life, is a reflection of all that is you. This is an absolute spiritual principle. To change the way someone treats you, change your limiting beliefs and repressed, damaging emotions. Then you will see a change in the people or circumstances around you. I will give you tools and methods in upcoming chapters to help you to recognize your beliefs and emotions and change to the ones you want.

Everyday, I see changes in my clients and how they relate to life. Often people come into sessions when they generally sense their life is not working and in some ways they feel powerless. Often they have been living as victims and they are unaware of their behavior.

When people allow abuse in their lives, they might not be standing up for themselves or defending their personal space and boundaries. As a coach I know they must feel unworthy. Once they start treating themselves better, loving themselves, and feeling their inner worth, they start to stand up for themselves, and their environment changes. They see for themselves that the abusive people or circumstances change or move on.

Creating Your Reality: An Example

One client, whom I'll call Mary, made major changes in her life when she started to realize and live her new understandings. Mary had been in one form of counseling or another for seven years before she came to my office. She had many health problems, her self-esteem was very low and she felt totally powerless. I saw her only eight times before she moved out of state. Mary had a deep desire to grow, which is absolutely necessary to achieve any change. She worked very hard with the principles I taught her and she diligently applied them to every aspect of her life.

Mary was brought up to believe she was a powerless victim and her body could never heal. She was surrounded by people who constantly invalidated her. Even in the different group therapies she attended, people reinforced helplessness, victimhood, and powerlessness. She was never told or made aware she could change her view of life to a more empowering one.

I helped her understand the concept of creating her own reality. In all her years of therapy, no one had ever asked her how she felt! So we worked to make it safe for her to feel and process her unconscious anger. Each session I saw a change in her. As she tried on new concepts, her life started to change. She started to stand up for herself and say no to people who overstepped her boundaries. She released old, negative, limiting relationships and started to attract more positive people. She began to rely on herself to nurture herself and get her needs met. This was something she didn't know she could do before! As her unconscious beliefs started to change, she began to see her health problems as temporary and fixable, instead of a way of life. She had an eating disorder and it went away. Her zest for life and energy increased. She was tremendously excited about living life from the higher spiritual consciousness because she felt, for the first time, a sense of purpose in living.

Mary is a perfect example of how you can change your environment by changing yourself. As Mary's inner beliefs changed, her awareness of life and how she reacted to it changed. This, in turn, changed her vibrational level, attracting people and situations that reflected this new consciousness. She started to look at life as her teacher, instead of something to just muddle through.

The exercises in the chapters "Love" and "Balance" should start you on your way to having better feelings about yourself. Allow yourself every vehicle to help you achieve the self-love that you may need, whether it's therapy, group counseling, or getting in touch with your spiritual self.

If you just open your heart to ask for the message, relationships with yourself and others are always teaching you. Spirit has put all the tools you need within your grasp. At different times you may need different tools. The key to growth and change is allowing yourself what you need in the present moment. Love yourself enough to be flexible and listen to your inner self. Remember, growth and happiness are ongoing. Your inner growth and expanding happiness require you to constantly monitor your beliefs and emotions. When you do this, you can be conscious of the beliefs and emotions that empower or limit your life. This is living your life consciously. If you choose not to monitor your thoughts and emotions, you live your life in a robotic, reactive way. Freedom and growth come when you choose to live with more conscious, uplifting actions.

Karmic Relationships

Have you ever sensed you have known someone before and wondered why you felt that way? More than likely, you knew that person in a previous life. You might be in a relationship now to learn from each other or heal old wounds. This is called a karmic relationship.

He or she may be in your life because one of you may need to make of some kind of restitution. Or, you may be together to help each other grow spiritually and to heal the actions of your past. The more loving or spiritual you were together in the past, the closer you may feel toward that individual now. Try to look at your relationships with all the people in your life as vehicles for your growth. Some karmic relationships can be intense. They can last any length of time, from a day to years.

The more you let Spirit guide you, the faster you grow. Your lessons are then sped up. The person who consistently separates herself or himself from other people usually has slower growth than someone who relates to others. Most lessons require relating to other people whether you knew them in past lives or not.

What is absolutely necessary for your growth is your willingness to clear or let go of limiting, negative actions, beliefs, and emotions, so Spirit can flow through you more clearly to affect you and others profoundly. If you refuse to relate to others or refuse to be honest with yourself in confronting what you need to do to change, the flow of Spirit and Divine Love is blocked. You can only grow so far. The very acts of confronting yourself and working through what you find changes your consciousness. Like Mary, you can grow more quickly if you are willing to boldly confront yourself with the reasons your life is the way it is.

Love Requires Action

Relationships are active when you help yourself and others at the same time. Loving is an active state! The higher your awareness, the more love you let flow through you and flow to others. Relationships help you become a more loving being.

As you grow spiritually, your lessons with different loved ones may manifest more quickly. At first this may cause conflict or disharmony. This disharmony is just a refinement of your vibrations as you evolve spiritually. It is similar to eating healthy foods or fasting when your previous diet was filled with unhealthy foods. Once you start refining your diet with healthier foods you may feel worse before you feel better. This is because the body now has the fuel to sweep all the toxins out of your body. So too as you grow spiritually, you will probably rid yourself of a little negative karma when you are with others.

People who are close usually have more lessons to learn from their relationship. In the instance of people who are married, the lessons from the relationship can be far more intense and far-reaching than those with casual acquaintances. The same holds true for family and good friends. Many times, when the spiritual lessons are over, people go on to new lessons with other people. As you grow, you may see different people come and go in your life, including spouses.

Growth Through Relationships

In my own life, a relationship that has meant tremendous growth for me is my relationship with a man named Paul. I met him at a seminar in Elmira, New York while we were both going through divorces.

When I first met him I was not immediately attracted to him. But as the seminar progressed I talked more with him, and I felt very drawn to him. In my dreams I experienced his energy and presence. Later I found out he experienced the same with me.

By the end of the seminar we were inseparable, and I was sad the seminar was ending. He decided to drive me to the airport so I could catch my flight home to Atlanta before he drove home to Toronto. On the way to the airport, he spontaneously decided to fly with me to Atlanta! Well, I think it's every woman's fantasy to be pursued, and I remember being flattered by his affection and attention.

In Atlanta, we spent four days together. I hadn't planned this, and I still had clients to see. But many clients cancelled during his stay, which gave us more time together. We had a great time and grew extremely close very quickly.

Paul had to go back to Toronto after a few days, and since we met right before Christmas, I decided to take my Christmas break with him in Canada. I spent ten great days in Toronto with him, and at the end of the ten days he asked me to marry him, and I said yes.

We both knew it was very fast, but our connection was extremely deep. I had never before connected this way with anyone else. Immediately, we started to plan to live together. We ended up choosing Atlanta as a place to live because I had an established practice, and Paul, an actor, could make a living in the states.

From January to April, we communicated often and saw each other as much as we could. We were flying back and forth and creating a lot of costly phone bills, and he wrote me the most beautiful letters! When he came down to Atlanta in April, we found a beautiful house and bought it together. He moved in that month and our intense life lessons began because our deep love for each other had opened the way for our healing to surface. Both of us had come from dysfunctional homes, and we had developed unhealthy ways of relating in our former marriages. Living together, we were aware of these facts and worked at eliminating unhealthy behaviors from our relationship.

We wanted to have a marriage free of co-dependency and to love each other in the unconditional way that makes it safe to be totally ourselves. We both wanted to be complete and happy individuals who didn't need the other to be happy, but we wanted to be with each other to share our wholeness. Both of us were concerned with growth, and we tried to always incorporate our spirituality into our daily lives. Our love and connection with Spirit opened the door for incredible healing for both of us, but not in the way you might expect. Paul found out his father had cancer. My father also had cancer, and they died about a month apart. We delayed our marriage, we rationalized, because of our fathers' deaths. Really, we were finding more lessons in our deeper selves that would require time apart.

In only a year, we both had gone through incredible losses. Paul got divorced and sold his farm, which was his life's dream. He left his country, and his father died. I got divorced, my cat — my dear friend of seventeen years — died, and my father died. These were just the outer changes. Internally we both were letting go of long-held negative beliefs about our own worth. We both grew a lot in knowing about love and its power to heal.

With Paul's love I was able to feel more secure and self-loving. I was able to give love to others without losing myself, though I knew I still had to let go of more layers of deeper internal fears and my tendency to have unhealthy relationships. Through our love, Paul felt safe enough to be more of himself, and he went through a lot of tough development and decision-making. He knew he loved me, but he also knew he had never given himself the space he needed for his own development.

For the next few months it was very difficult. Paul was trying to decide if he should marry me or go back to Canada. I was feeling his indecision, and I tried not to force him to stay. I believe that when you love someone you shouldn't manipulate that person to do what you want him or her to do. Still, it was extremely hard for me to come to terms with Paul's indecision.

Paul finally decided not to get married and to go back to Canada. I was devastated at first. It took a lot for me to get over that, but the changes in me, my growth, and inner peace were tremendous, because I made a decision to evolve through the experience. Even though it was painful, we both were better off knowing each other than if we never met.

Spirit and Healing

I believe that Spirit put us together to help each other heal our past, internalized issues. Our relationship was intense, loving, and growth-oriented — deep and healing on all levels. I had, over the year we were together, many dreams about us that represented our growth together and revealed to me former lives I had spent with him. Through these dreams, I realized I had known Paul in many, many lifetimes that went way, way back in time.

I grew lifetimes through knowing and loving Paul. Even though we broke up, I felt the relationship was a spiritual success. We grew in our capacity to love. By loving ourselves and sharing a deep love, the relationship was truly a success!

Levels of Relating

It is up to you to choose how to deal with people in your life. Relationships can be dealt with on many levels. You can approach life and people in your life from a limited or limitless viewpoint. When you put Spirit first in your life, you will relate to people in the most effective way for your and their growth. When you live in this way, you are coming from a limitless, higher purpose for living.

The only unchanging thing in life is Spirit, which is Divine Love. The more you love yourself and others, the more you will get in touch with that which is changeless, that which is real. The foremost relationship to nurture is the one with you, Spirit, and God.

I try to live my life integrating my spiritual self with all the rest of me. All the people who come into my life, from the most significant to the most incidental, are in my life for a purpose. I am choosing to learn from all people.

In my romantic relationships, I have seen myself change from relating to men on merely a physical level to a more complete level, like my relationship with Paul. As I focus on spiritual growth and view other people as Soul needing particular experiences in their journeys of growth, my life and my relationships have gotten better and more rewarding.

Releasing Attachments

The unhealthy ways I related to others and myself is dropping away faster now because I realize that I am not responsible for other people's happiness or growth. Previously I might have tried to force advice or help people "for their own good." I now realize others may need a particular lesson (that might entail some suffering) for their spiritual growth. I am getting better at not forcing my views on others. If I offer advice now and it isn't taken, I can understand others are entitled to their own opinions.

It's not that I don't care about people. I wouldn't have written this book if I didn't care. It's that I am now trying to release attachments regarding what my ego might think is better for someone else's life. When I live in this way, I not only grow and get what's best for me — I let others grow in ways that are perfect for them as Soul.

Sometimes living your life for the good of all means separation. Other times it might mean you will be with someone for the rest of your life. Spirit knows what's best, not your ego. If I had held tightly to Paul and manipulated him to stay because I thought it was best, I am sure our growth and happiness would have stopped. My first husband Greg had doubts just like Paul. Then, my ego took hold and I forced the situation because I believed I was right. Through my ego, I was trying to control another. Even though Greg had free will and could have left at any time, I believe my energy influenced him to marry me when he really didn't want to.

Greg and I are good friends, but in many painful ways we were not right for each other. I believe our conflicts kept arising so we could come to terms with what we needed to learn. My ego wanted my life to be a certain way, but if I had come from a deeper spiritual awareness at that time, I believe we would have separated sooner because we would have passed through our lessons faster. Maybe we would never have married.

I learned more in my year with Paul than in any previous time in my life. I consistently grow and feel happier. Some people will be in my life a short time, while others will be in it for my whole life. I am learning that the time frame of relationships is not as important as the lessons learned from them.

Forgiveness and Non-judgment

Two important keys that have helped me form better relationships with others and myself are forgiveness and non-judgment. They are very similar. Forgiveness is an attitude that is important to cultivate when you feel that you have been wronged. Being non-judgmental is an ongoing process. When you are non-judgmental and forgiving, you attain a higher consciousness.

Most people feel forgiveness means pardoning another person for an error or indiscretion. That view comes from the small ego. It implies you are above someone else, that you are the judge. True forgiveness means you reach a point in consciousness that you realize no one is to blame for anything; no one is wrong. Whatever happens in a relationship is perfect for what you need as Soul to grow. In the deeper understanding of life, there is no one to forgive; whatever happens in your life is perfect.

Forgiveness means that eventually, if you are linked with your higher self and Spirit, you will consciously realize whatever transpired was perfect for your growth. You are then able to release all attachments to how you wanted a situation to turn out and all negative energy regarding that event or person. Then true impartial love can flow through you and from you.

Processing Your Emotions

This doesn't mean you won't have feelings when things happen to you or that you can't defend your boundaries if necessary. I definitely had strong feelings about Paul that I needed to process when we broke up. If I had kept thinking that Paul wronged me, my life's energy would have created negativity and affected my whole life negatively. I went through feelings of anger and sadness to process my loss, but I came to understand there was no one to blame and what happened was perfect. In this understanding, I did not deny my emotions. I processed them through the stages of loss — denial, anger, sadness, and resolution — to facilitate my growth.

When I use the word "process" regarding your emotions, I mean you allow your emotions healthy avenues of expression to transform your emotional energy so that you can clearly be in the present moment. You bring them up to your consciousness to clear. When you repress your emotions or you express them without resolving why you feel the way you do, you stop your growth. For example, if I had stayed angry with Paul or let myself stay sad, I could never have gotten on with my life. My emotional self would still have been in the relationship. Consequently, to go forward in my life, I had to allow myself to feel all the emotions necessary to process my grief over ending our relationship.

Overcoming Judgments and Facilitating Forgiveness

When you live with an attitude of forgiveness and non-judgment, it is easier to heal your emotional self because you are beginning to live your life from a higher awareness. The more judgments you remove from your thinking, the better your relationships will become with everyone, including yourself. When you release judgments, you open your heart to Divine Love on every level of your being.

Being non-judgmental is an attitude of tolerance. Being judgmental negatively affects every relationship you have, including the one with yourself. When you judge yourself or others on how they live, you are coming from your ego. You are saying your way of living is right or your way of being is the only way. Judgments with your attitude and energy create blocks in relationships. If you are judging, you think your way is the only way of doing, being, or having. Judging also includes attitudes or thoughts that you have about a person for something he or she is, did, or has.

Being a human being means you will have opinions. Know that you are entitled to your opinions, but also know that preferences and opinions are different than judgments. I may like the color blue (a preference) but I try not to tell others or hold the attitude that blue is the only "right" color (a judgment).

Your goal is to clear away obstructions in your thinking or actions that keep Divine Love and Spirit from flowing through you to yourself and others. Judgments are energy blocks that keep you from growing and loving.

I am going to leave you with a contemplation to increase your love for others and help you overcome judgments and facilitate forgiveness, thus improving your relationships.

Exercise

Overcoming Judgments

Get in a comfortable sitting position. Close your eyes and gently focus your attention on the area between your eyes. Chant the word HU this time, because HU opens your heart up to Divine Love. Chant HU for ten to twenty minutes and bring up as much of a feeling of love as you can. Visualize yourself surrounded with blue light, which represents Divine Love. Now picture the people you have relationships with and what you would like to heal or address with them. See either Angels or other highly evolved loving beings moving about you and the other people. You and the others are surrounded by Divine Light and protected by the beings of love. Imagine the people peeling off their physical bodies and see them now as brilliant bodies of light. Realize that their true selves are Soul. Now peel off your body and with it all the negative energy, thoughts, and judgments you may have about them or their situations. See all of you surrounded by the Light and Divine Love of God.

You may have to do this contemplation (or one of your own) many times. NEVER try to direct the Light or Sound to change another person. Your aim is to get to a place of peace within yourself about a particular person or relationship. (You can even do this for yourself to feel your true self is Soul, not just this body or ego.) The more actions you take to relate to yourself and others from the belief and viewpoint of your spiritual self, the more this life makes sense and the more complete you will feel.

Forgiveness

Here's another way to do this contemplation. Once again chant HU for ten to twenty minutes. Then see the person you have problems with. Say, "I forgive you for anything that you may have done to me in the past, present, or future. I also forgive myself for anything I may have done to you in the past, present, or future." These statements, made with sincerity and feeling, are incredibly powerful and can help you to eliminate negativity between yourself and the other person. ↶

Relating is an ongoing process. Try to remember to relate to others and yourself in a vibrant and ever loving way. As you take actions to relate to life, yourself, and others in this fashion, a new dimension and depth to your life will emerge. I promise you will feel a new aliveness and joy with more and more people, including yourself! Be true to yourself and shoot for the highest you possibly can be. All that is good for your life will manifest!

CHAPTER SIX

Love

*Love is the power
that heals,
uplifts,
brings joy and light
into your life.*

*Love is the power
that creates
All
that is beautiful, abundant,
and good.*

*Love is the power.
When nurtured,
it
Changes the course
of your life.*

*Love is the power.
As you accept it
from Spirit,
you can accomplish
ANYTHING!*

The human race has a deep fascination with love. Love is constantly on people's minds. It's the subject of countless songs, books, and movies. Love is the most precious and beautiful experience you can have! Love is also the most mysterious and confusing of your emotions.

In this chapter I'll try to explain what love is, clarify how you can attain more of it in your life, and, eventually, how to evolve your love to the highest form and express it in the purest way.

What is Love?

In your lifetime you will experience many kinds of love. There is the love parents have for their children, love for one's lover or mate, love that you have for friends, and so on. But what is love? People say they are experiencing love or that they are in love. But what is this emotion we all call love?

This question takes me to an experience I had at a spiritual seminar that was designed to help the individual grow toward God in one's own unique way. I was attending this seminar with all my best friends and my sister Joan. I knew when I got back home I was going to start writing this chapter, so my mind was focused on love. We had been at this seminar for three days, and on the last day we had brunch together before leaving for home.

During brunch, the question "What is love?" popped into my mind. Because I wanted a little feedback, I asked that question of everyone at the table.

I was feeling uneasy about this chapter. Understanding love is so important, and I wanted to convey this understanding as clearly as possible.

My friends adore talking about the different aspects of life and growth — we all are passionate about this kind of communication. So now you have all these people who have been spirituality submerged for three days, who adore talking about life as much as they need to breathe, and when I asked them about love they ignored my question. This was out of character for everyone there; consequently, their lack of response had a powerful impact on me.

I have been working with Spirit long enough to feel their lack of response was not out of rudeness or insensitivity. I felt it was Spirit's way of teaching me I already had the answer. The waking dream that rang true for me was that each individual has an inner awareness of what love is. We all have answers inside ourselves as Soul. Love may mean different things to different people at different times.

I am learning more each day to always look to Spirit to guide me in my life. I believe my writing this book has been guided by Spirit, and that the incident during our brunch was a lesson for me about trusting my intuition and Spirit. No matter how much I prodded, I couldn't get anyone to answer my question. I think love is impossible to put into words. A true and deep understanding of love is a knowing and an experience that comes from your heart and Soul.

This makes my job even harder. I am writing a chapter about something that can't be known with words! Instead of giving a definition of love, I'm going to describe some basic characteristics of love and the different kinds of love you can experience.

Loving Yourself

The first avenue of expressing love is for your self. The deepest aspect of self-love is giving and opening your heart to Spirit or God and letting the wonderful light energy flow through your being. On a more human level it is loving your flaws and imperfections through all your life lessons. When you love and accept yourself fully, every aspect of your life flourishes. I just can't emphasize self-love enough!

If your heart is closed to yourself, how can it be open for others? Your heart is the gateway of and to God and Spirit. Self-love is the food and the seed of all other love and positive things in your life.

Many people believe self-love is negative selfishness. I definitely disagree. When you open your heart to loving yourself you are opening the way to a deeper connection to God (who is Divine Love ITSELF) and ultimately to a deep love and positive energy for all of life. How can opening your heart to God and Spirit be bad? How can raising your vibrations be anything but good?

Too many people try to attain self-love by relating to others in a way that doesn't appear negative, but really is. Let's take the example of a person who has not yet healed his or her inner emotional traumas. This person might compensate for a lack of self-love by always giving to others. Giving to others is noble. I am not discounting the act of giving. But the *true* reason this person may be giving is because *unconsciously* he or she feels unloved. In this example, by giving to others, the person is trying to get love that he or she has not received or given to him or her self. When a person does this, they are feeding a deep need.

Some people unconsciously feel that if they give enough, then they are worthwhile, and they will receive love. When, in fact, only when you love yourself fully first can you freely give to others. Self-love is not sitting around and adoring yourself — that's not love, that's negative energy from the ego. When you experience deep self-love you have the energy and the desire to serve Spirit through your unique, individual life. Self-love is an ongoing evolution and expansion that spills over to everyone in your life, without losing yourself in the process. When you are in touch with the source of love and consistently fill yourself up with it, you have an endless supply of love for all of life and you are a part of the whole of life you need to love!

Love as Energy

Love is a condition of positive, fulfilled consciousness. Since love is energy, it needs to flow, just like a stream or river needs to flow to be pure. When you are in the *highest* state of loving, you are an open vehicle for the Light and Sound of the Holy Spirit to flow through you without ego attachments. You are both giving and receiving. If you are energy, everything about you vibrates or moves, because the intrinsic nature of energy is movement. If, in your own life, you are vibrating from lack (in this case, the lack of love), when your energy intermingles with others, it will be vibrating from a state of lack. If you are in this state while you are in a romance, a friendship, or family structure, you, in truth, want something from the other people. You want their love energy to fill an emptiness within you. So in a very true sense, you are taking something from them. You are not giving or being a truly open vehicle for Spirit, as you might believe.

Taking someone else's energy is not a pure form of love. If you have complete self-love, you give to others with no expectation of wanting anything from them, while at the same time you protect your own boundaries and fulfill your own needs. You are able to do this because you have more than enough love flowing through your life already. You have to realize your own love in your life before you can share it successfully with anyone else. **You cannot give something you don't already possess!**

Opening Your Heart

People usually find it very hard to open their hearts to deep self-love or to God and Spirit. A connection with God is not something that our society focuses on outside of a few hours on Sunday, but it **needs** to be a daily focus and practice. A large way you connect to God is through self-love, which is part of Divine Love. Divine love is limitless, just as God is limitless. Because your truest nature is Spiritual, when you close off your heart to yourself, you close off your heart to Spirit and God.

There may be people who can open their hearts to others and in the process have their own hearts open to themselves. But I find more individuals having problems because of a lack of self-love, rather than the other way around.

Why Self-love Is Important

Self-love opens your heart to God and balances you emotionally, mentally, and physically. You allow yourself to rest when you need to rest, and you have fun when you need to have fun. Self-love is not abusing yourself with guilt when you are giving yourself what you need. Self-love expresses itself in positive appreciation for your own uniqueness and feeling your worth as Soul. Self-love and self-worth are closely tied together. It's hard to feel worthy if you don't love yourself.

In my own life, I find that the more I love and respect myself, the more I am truly able to give love from my heart to others, without strings attached, and the more good I can receive without guilt. When I felt unworthy, I had no energy or love to give to others. I blocked all the good that was available to me. My relationships with men were unhealthy, and I tried to get my worth and internal self-love from their approval. Taking responsibility for others and negating myself for a man's love was my way of trying to get love and worth for myself. If I already had love internally, I wouldn't have put up with the abuse I attracted. I would have respected myself no matter what and allowed myself to be around people who also respected me.

The more love I allow myself by connecting with Spirit, the deeper and more satisfying my relationships are with all people. When the core of my being is connected to Spirit, I have love energy to give without having to draw other people's energy back into myself. Because of this connection to Spirit and Divine Love within myself, I have a balance between my inflow and my outflow through Spirit, others, and myself. With this balanced love flow you will find your life growing more joyful and rich.

Exercise

Loving Yourself More Fully

To love yourself more fully, you have to know what parts of yourself are shut off from love. This exercise will help you pinpoint parts of yourself that need love and care for.

Take a piece of paper and draw a line down the middle. On the left side of the paper, list all parts of yourself you dislike, hate, or ignore. These parts can be body parts, emotional ways of dealing with life, or aspects of your intelligence. Other parts might be your male or female sides of your adult self, your inner child, and so on. For example, if you have a hard time asserting yourself, this could be an indication of not loving your male side. This can be true whether you are a male or female, for we all have both aspects. Another example: If you have difficulty having fun, you may have been ignoring your inner-child, or your inner-child may need more love. Really take some time with this, and let yourself know what you need. Be honest and non-shaming toward what you find.

On the right side of the paper, list all the aspects of yourself that you like and consciously know that you love.

Now set aside at least twenty minutes of uninterrupted time. Put on some soothing music. (Music can powerfully impact of your imagery.)

Imagine a very safe place. It can be a room, nature setting or a spiritual setting. Feel safe and secure and open for growth. Visualize yourself meeting all the parts you listed on the left hand side of the paper. One by one, send them love and thank them all because on some level they have helped you survive. Validate the job they have done. You are validating their effort, *not the effect. It is similar to*

> *getting a really awful gift from someone you care*
> *about. You sincerely thank them for their effort and*
> *intention, NOT their taste. You do the same thing*
> *with your parts. Keep in mind that on some level*
> *they were trying to help you. When you are sincere*
> *in your appreciation you will notice a shift in your*
> *feelings about each part. Maybe when you thanked*
> *them, you imagined your eyes shining brighter, or*
> *maybe when you thanked them, your thighs in*
> *your visualization got smaller or you felt lighter in*
> *your heart. Keep doing this until you can sense or*
> *feel more acceptance for yourself.* ⌒

Doing this exercise can help you accept yourself and create the love you want. You may uncover beliefs that were hindering your growth. By releasing negative beliefs, you open yourself to healthier relationships with others. The more you love yourself, the more love you allow into your life from others.

Understanding Love

When you block loving yourself or receiving love from others, the flow of love is out of balance, and someone, either you or another, becomes a victim. This is especially true with romantic love, because your boundaries are difficult to keep in place. You cannot continue to stay balanced and grow healthily if you give romantic or emotional love to someone who does not return your love. Love, like any energy, needs to continually move and flow. So if another person does not accept your love, love is blocked from flowing.

Romantic Love

Most of us have experienced romantic love. It starts when you meet someone and all the boundaries between the two of you come down. In the first stages, the other person seems perfect in most every way. There is a balanced flow of energy; each person is giving and receiving love energy on the personal, emotional, intellectual, and (in some cases) even the spiritual level. Interpersonal, individual, emotional, mental, and spiritual growth can be best achieved when both people are open, giving, and receiving, on all levels.

Ultimately I feel the truest and highest reason two people are in a romantic relationship is to grow spiritually. When we have a romantic relationship with someone, especially in marriage, many doors are open for learning, healing, and growing. Love opens the way for growth!

When Love is Blocked

But if strong love energy becomes blocked at either end, the people in the relationship can suffer. This blockage can occur when either party no longer wants to communicate or grow with the same depth or speed as the other. Personal love — romantic love—needs an opening for energy to be received and given. If a blockage occurs, the best way to salvage the relationship is to restructure it to be one of impersonal Divine Love. The person in the relationship who wants more romantic love should stop giving intense romantic love because the other person is not ready to exchange the love or accept love in the romantic, personal way.

Now, personally, I try never to tell someone else what to do. With this example, I am suggesting actions one can take to go forward. No one knows what experiences another may need to grow toward God. Some people may need this experience to understand how the flow of love works or for other lessons as Soul. If you experience this, contemplate the best course of action for yourself.

Love Needs Action to Grow

Love, whether personal or divine, requires continual action to grow. Love is not a nice warm fuzzy or a place where you arrive and languish. You need to continually give to yourself what you need. A healthy relationship may have ups and downs. Each party needs to act to keep the love flowing. When each individual is committed to health, growth, and love of self and the other, only good can occur.

When you realize there is no hope of equal exchange, the pattern of love needs to change. The time frame for realizing a relationship has changed is different for all relationships. If you continue to give emotional, romantic love to someone who cannot reciprocate, you become a victim. You are using your power or energy passively. Your relationship becomes a one-way street. You create negative actions when you consistently send energy or personal love to someone who cannot or will not receive it. You are invading their personal space and over-stepping their emotional boundary.

Your life will reflect this in many ways. Maybe constant arguments or disharmony will manifest in your relationship. If you are the one sending out the unwanted love, you may feel powerless and lose energy, or something will feel off-kilter in your life or as a couple.

Loving from Personal Power

A relationship or love exchange comes from a positive place when both parties are at cause in their life, when each person comes from a place of personal power. When I use the word "power" here or anywhere in this book, I am referring to a state of consciousness of connecting with Spirit in creating your life. This means you are at cause in your life, consciously taking actions to create your life with the most value without trying to control others. Relationships can then grow in positive ways with harmonious effects for all parties.

Look to the workings of your daily life to know how love is flowing in your life. You become powerless when you want and wait for another person's love, and it is not forthcoming. You are at the mercy of their actions and have relinquished your power of creating. Losing personal power causes suffering in romantic relationships and can happen in other personal relationships as well. This does not make anyone wrong; it could be an indication of tremendous growth for all concerned. Everyone needs different experiences to grow, and many times when you are growing the most, your relationships change quickly. You may be experiencing lessons with another person in a year or two that otherwise would take a lifetime.

Learning from Love

Let me give you an example. In the beginning, when Paul and I exchanged personal love, our energy and our commitment to us as individuals and as a couple had an even flow to it. During our first few months together, we were both receivers and givers of love. When Paul moved to Atlanta (and maybe even before that time), there was a subtle shift in his energy and attention to the relationship as a whole. I felt the change immediately, but I denied it because I didn't want it to happen. At first I felt that it was because he moved from his own country to a new city and country. Around this same time, he found out his father was ill. I felt all these things were affecting him, but they were not. He was withdrawing his romantic love from our relationship, as I found out later, for the growth of his self as Soul.

In the physical realm, there is a difference in the kind of love one gives. When individuals are not clear about the differences, personal boundaries, and expectations, it causes problems. Paul needed time outside a committed relationship to grow. Even though he loved me, he was not able to commit to me or to our relationship for the long-term relationship and marriage I wanted.

This period in our lives was very confusing for both of us; we loved each other, yet we each had to take actions that were the best for our individual growth. While Paul sorted out what was best for his growth as Soul, I felt him withdraw his energy from me and from us as a couple. This change in him shifted how we could relate.

At first I tried to give more romantic love and, at the same time, give him space. The more I gave romantic love to him when he was not capable of receiving it or reciprocating, the more I felt alone and rejected. Later, I learned the more I gave, the more he felt smothered. I was operating from effect, the powerless stance of being a victim. This is always negative. ("Negative" in that it doesn't come from your personal power as a creator.) Because I was operating from the negative, my energy was being drained in every way. This drain affected my work, my health, and my creativity. No one was causing this drain but me.

The Importance of Balanced Love Flow

At that time there was not a balanced flow of energy between Paul and me. A separation of energies such as we had was a major breakdown of two people relating as a couple. As time passed, I had to face the reality that Paul needed to go his own way.

I had to realize there was no longer an exchange of the kind of deep and romantic love that was necessary for our relationship to work out. Paul needed to shut off accepting that kind of love from me, and I suffered greatly. His closing his heart to me in this way was not something I wanted to live with. I thought it might take years for him to want to work as a couple. We both understood that to keep giving out love energy that can't be reciprocated is unhealthy for both parties.

If I had continued to give him romantic love when he could not reciprocate, I would have been a victim. Remember, victims are powerless in their lives because they do not claim their spiritual power to create the lives they want. I had to shift from loving Paul romantically to giving him an impersonal, spiritual kind of love. I now had to give him Divine Love only if I wanted to be happy and healthy.

When I started to switch my romantic love energy to one coming from just one Soul loving another Soul, I started reclaiming my power. I needed to relinquish my *attachment* to a romantic connection. You can only grow when you are in the consciousness of being at cause (a creator), and not at effect (a victim). Remember, actions made from personal power create value for your growth and self-worth. When I started to be at cause and reclaim my power over my own life, my suffering lessened.

That time was tremendously powerful. Both of us implemented self-love, which helped us heal inner issues about childhood. The more you allow self-love to grow, even in romantic relationships, the more positive the outcome will be for the overall growth of your life.

Flow of Love

I feel most people do not realize how important keeping an open flow with regards to love and energy can be, and they suffer because they are unaware of how energy affects their lives. If you give personal energy — emotions, thoughts, and actions — to people with an attitude of attachment to its outcome or to people who are incapable of receiving this energy, you will suffer.

Everything you do, feelings included, is affected on this plane of existence by cause and effect. Every action has a reaction. If you keep putting water into a container and the container has no way to be emptied, the water will spill out and probably cause a mess. This is an example of energy that is blocked from flowing. The same holds true when you give personal energy to others who are incapable or unwilling to receive it, only you find the mess is in your own life. Remember that energy needs to keep moving.

Problems of Attachment

You may be unaware of imbalances in your life caused by your attachment to or persistent flow of your energy to another person. This type of imbalance is in fact a disregard for another person's boundaries. You are forcing part of yourself into someone's space without his or her permission. That is why it is negative. You must have the other person's permission or willingness to receive your love or energy to have a positive relationship and effect in your life. This permission comes very rarely with words. You have to watch and observe their actions and reactions to your giving. Remember that actions always speak louder than words.

Personal Love and Divine Love

So many of us are taught to give personal love strongly to people we feel are needy and we are taught to give our personal love whether the other person abuses it or not. Romantic love and other kinds of personal love come from parts of your lower self, like the emotional body or mind. These forms of love carry attachments regarding an outcome. Since you are energy, you give your energy when you give personal love to others. When others can't accept it or when they abuse your gift, the flow is stopped and you could suffer because of this. It is similar to trying to fill a bottle with water when the bottle has a lid on it. The water will go everywhere except in the bottle.

Divine Love is like sunshine on the bottle of water. Even when the lid is on the bottle, sunlight can get through. Sunlight passing through a bottle with a lid *does not interfere* with the bottle or the water. The sunlight represents the limitless source, power, and detachment of Divine Love.

I am in total agreement with giving impersonal or Divine Love to all. When you give Divine Love, you are expressing love not from your human consciousness or the wants of your ego, but from yourself as Soul. When you express love in this way, the love energy aligns with Spirit and God. It is given freely without attachments.

When I talk about Divine Love, I mean giving love from a place in Soul that is in union with Spirit and God. It is a place where personal energy is not going to be abused or used. Divine Love is a gift from God through one person to another. It is impersonal and unattached. The more personal or romantic the love becomes, the more careful you have to be not to overstep people's boundaries or become attached or dependent.

Techniques of Opening Up to Love

The first step in creating anything, including love, is to know you can create it. Knowing you have the power to create is fundamental. Without this knowing, you are left without hope and direction.

If the direction in your life is to achieve more love in your outer world, you have to start with changing your inner world. **Change always moves from inner to outer.** When you change your inner self, your outer environment changes. This is why self-love has to come first, so you can manifest more love in your outer life.

To make a comprehensive change in your life, it is better to use every level — Soul, the mind (conscious and unconscious), the emotions, and the physical body — to achieve that change. When you use these parts in unison, you manifest your desires faster.

Importance of Sincerity

An important aspect of creating more love in your life is sincerity. This is the state of consciousness that Christ talked about when he spoke of being like a little child. Sincerity goes right to your depths, right to Soul, right through to Spirit. It is the big open eyes of a child, open to see everything. It is trust, letting down the ego barriers of the small self, and openly stating that what you want in your life is the deep Divine Love of Spirit. Sincerity means that you are not too grown up, too smart, or too knowledgeable to want this state of consciousness. It's a wanting and a hunger from your heart for the flow of Divine Love to enter your being.

What follows are different exercises to help you open different aspects of yourself so you can accept more love into your life on every level. When you use these exercises, follow your intuition. Maybe for one day or for a few weeks, you will be using one exercise. Then it may become clear to you to stop that exercise and use another. Trust your instincts.

For instance, maybe you've realized that the flow of love is stopped because of a belief you've been holding about your self-worth. If so, the exercises dealing with the mind might be appropriate. Or maybe you are frozen emotionally, with fears you can't pinpoint. If that were the case, the best exercises would be ones that deal with your emotional body. Allow yourself to know what you need to achieve change so you can acquire love. The love you seek is already in your life as Soul, but your blocks keep you from experiencing love fully in the present moment.

Exercise

How to Expand Love

Any exercise in this book can help you open up to yourself as Soul and connect you with Spirit in a greater way. Working with high vibratory words consistently each day is an extremely powerful tool to do just this. When you chant or sing the words, focus on your heart area. Do not direct the Sound; just open your heart to Spirit's energy and Divine Love.

If that were your whole spiritual practice, it would be sufficient to connect with the Holy Spirit. But because we're human, our minds get bored and we need diversity. After you have sung your word for a few minutes you may want to try this visualization. You can still silently sing your word as you visualize. Imagine your heart area as a ball of shimmering light. See that ball expanding, radiating outward past your physical body. Expand your heart light as far as you can imagine, past your room, your house, throughout the world. Let the Light be Divine Love. Be as detached as you can be to how Divine Love affects life and what IT touches. Be open to receive the love of this Light yourself! Do this for about twenty minutes a day and take notice of how your life changes for the better on various levels.

Exercise

Affirmations

Another powerful tool is affirmations. Affirmations are tools to help you create something that is not yet in your life. Writing them every day is the most powerful way to use them. Always write them in the present tense, as the subconscious mind knows only the present.

When you write your affirmations, notice how you feel in your body. If you feel tension, restructure how you write the affirmation. For example, if you had a broken leg and wrote, "My leg is healed," you probably will feel tense in your body and your self-talk would be, "yeah, right." While you are in the process of creating with affirmations you have to feel comfortable with them on every level. A better way to structure that affirmation about your broken leg would be, "My leg is healing more and more each day." This affirmation helps your conscious mind feel comfortable while the rest of you helps to create this reality.

Affirmations won't work if you are scared or feel unworthy. Therefore two powerful ways to start any affirmation are, "I am safe" or "I am worthy." Then proceed with the rest of your affirmation.

Here are some affirmations to help you grow spiritually and develop Divine Love in your life:

"I am safe and worthy to receive the Light and Sound of God."

"More and more each day, I am accepting Divine Love from the Holy Spirit."

"I am safe to let the love of God flow through me."

"I am worthy of God's love NOW."

"I am safe and worthy to love myself."

"I am open to receive and live the Divine will of God."

"I am now safe to release my emotional and mental blocks to a joyful and loving life."

See what you want create in your life or what has been missing and make up your own affirmations. Starting today write them out in longhand each day. Take one and write it fifteen times once a day. Repetition speeds up the process of creation. ∽

Something you can do for your physical self that will help you open up to love is to act as if you are love. Start using your body in loving ways. Remember, there is no separation between your body, mind, and emotions. Actions on any level affect all parts of your self.

Acting As Love

Creating more love in your life is a process of action, not just feeling. After you have worked with your affirmations and spiritual contemplations, bring the awareness and love you have created into your daily life. Acts of kindness and the simple act of smiling to people can change your level of joy and make you a wonderful vehicle for more Divine Love in this world.

One day while you are doing your daily chores or working, focus on your heart and just send out love energy to life, without attachment, not directing it in any way. Just let it flow like the sun's rays flow through that bottle of water — the rays falling where they may. When you put love into action, you can see changes in your life.

I think these two quotes from Paul Twitchell's "Stranger by the River," sums up what I am trying to say. "Love is not a matter of belief. It is a matter of demonstration. It is not a question of authority, but one of perception and action." "Therefore, if you desire love, try to realize that the only way to get love is by giving love. The more you give, the more you get; and the only way in which you can give is to fill yourself with it, until you become a magnet of love."

Allow love to flow through you as well as to others. When you allow it to flow through you and outward in a detached way, you increase the amount of love you are capable of experiencing. It is similar to exercising your body; the more you move your body, the better and healthier your body gets. The more you let your body atrophy, the less it is capable of doing. The more actions you make toward accepting love within yourself and allowing it to flow outward, the more love will grow in your own heart.

The very action of asking for more love will lead you to manifest this love. Trust, and take action consistently. Open your heart and let it be filled with the love that you seek. **Love is nowhere else but inside you!**

CHAPTER SEVEN

Balance

It drives you crazy
Going from this to that
up and then down
inside and then out.
Peddling as fast as you can,
to find out that you
are already there
or didn't need to go.

Total juggling act.
At times all is in
perfect harmony and peace,
but once again you are on your way.
Growth ever-calling your name
having to rearrange once again
what is up, what is down
and what have you found . . .
That balance is not a stagnant state,
nothing never to be disturbed,
but a consistent rearrangement
of the ever-growing you.

W ithout balance you cannot experience the best life you are capable of because some part of you will be ineffective or overcompensating. Most people don't know what balance is and how important it is to the overall quality of their life. Let me explain how balance relates to every aspect of your life.

Being human means you are composed of many bodies, integral yet separate. You can readily understand you have a physical body, but there's more. Think of the mind, emotions, and Soul as separate bodies — or parts — of you. These parts comprise the total you. All these parts have different needs.

It is much easier to understand what you need as a person and how to get your needs met when you understand the functions and needs of each separate part. You are Soul first and foremost. Soul then takes on a physical body, the mind (which includes the conscious and unconscious), and the emotional self for this Earthly experience.

All these separate parts — spiritual, emotional, and mental — are linked together through Soul. They are not truly separate from your whole being or your physical self though they do need separate and direct care. When you act from a spiritual understanding that your truest, indestructible self is Soul, you can function more fully in this physical dimension.

Keeping the whole of you in balance is tremendously important for self-growth and self-mastery because when you are in balance, you are more open to Spirit flowing through you. If one or more of your bodies is out of balance, it keeps you from being conscious and aware of your higher self. It is important to consider all of your parts for the completion of your highest development.

Balance is another name for harmony. Without harmony you are fighting within yourself. If you are out of balance, you cannot grow as you could when every part of you is unified and nurtured. It is like the saying, "a house divided against itself cannot stand." When you know the requirements of each part, you can furnish exactly what each needs to heal and grow while staying unified. With this unification, tremendous joy, strength, and depth develop in your life.

You are the most effective and you can achieve the most in your life when all parts of you are happy and healthy. If you decide not to take care of yourself as a whole, you live with the consequences of being less than you could be. You don't have to do anything. You have free will, but you will always receive the consequences of your choices in life. This holds true for how you treat all the different parts of yourself as well.

The Physical Body

The most obvious part of you is your physical body. Even though it is the part most people relate to easily, it is still woefully neglected. Most of us were brought up with the belief there is always a doctor or pill to fix what ails you. This breeds a lack of responsibility toward your body and how you treat it.

Therefore what is a balanced body, and what can you do to facilitate health and harmony in your body? How can you learn to maintain and improve your health without becoming a doctor or studying nutrition for years?

Let me state right here, I'm not a physician or nutritionist. My suggestions are just that, suggestions. Ultimately, each individual has to find out what is correct for his or her personal health and well-being. What I offer are suggestions from my own experiences — what has worked for me — and suggestions from nutritionists and health professionals. You can use this information in your life if it seems correct to you. What is most important is for you to take an *active* role in your health.

Being Aware of What You Need

My awareness of health started when I observed my mother. She was sick for my whole life. Her sickness made me very aware that without health you really can't give to anyone fully or be all you want to be. When I ran away from home, I was a mess emotionally. I abused my body with cigarettes, drugs, and alcohol, and I was a full-blown bulimic. Needless to say, it was not a balanced lifestyle! Before I left home, I didn't realize how much control I could have regarding my health.

My older brother Marty planted seeds of understanding nutrition and self-responsibility regarding my health. He was into supplements, pure water, and exercise way before it was popular. At that time we all thought he was a little strange to take all those supplements and spend time exercising, but now I do a lot of what he was doing then.

At twenty-one, I felt I was an old forty. I was constantly without energy and always getting sick, especially with bronchitis. Following Marty's example, I started to pursue health, energy, and vitality. As I learned about cause and effect and started to incorporate it into my daily life, I realized that how I treated my body **did** make a difference. One of the first things I did was to quit smoking. Quitting smoking wasn't easy, but it was important for my health, and it started me on the road to a healthier way of life.

In trying to find a healthier and more balanced physical self, I learned our bodies do need all the basics. We need to drink plenty of clean water each day. We need quiet time, like contemplation. We need to eat more raw fruits and vegetables than cooked food. The body needs to be exercised regularly and exposed to fresh air and sunlight. This is not startling news to anyone. As you may already have concluded, the truths of life are very simple, but following these truths consistently can be difficult.

Everyone's body chemistry is different, and your requirements may be different than others in order for you to maintain balanced health. This is because each individual in every aspect is always changing. You will know if a food or an exercise is right for you because with it you will start to feel clearer, happier, or more energized. It is that simple. The key to having a healthier body is observing the simple cause-and-effect relationships in your life. Your observations will give you many answers to your life problems, even down to the basics of what kinds of food and exercise are right for you.

I listen to my body and observe how it feels at different times. I pay attention to what happens to it with the types of food I eat, how it feels after different kinds of exercise, and when it needs rest. I have learned that lots of sugar or junk foods detract from my energy, and emotionally I feel down when I eat too much of these foods. Exercise is vital for me to stay energized and mentally happy. Personally, I need lots of sunlight and lots and lots of water or I just feel lousy. I am aware that if I work too much indoors, sitting with clients or writing, my body starts to ache.

Because I have taken responsibility for my vitality and health for years, I look younger now than I did five years ago, and I have more energy and mental clarity than ever. I hardly ever get sick!

As I progress in my search for health and a balanced

body, there are some things I no longer do that I did before, and some things I'll keep doing. Personal health is the responsibility of each individual. What might be marvelous for me might not be great for you. What might be good for you now may not be right for you in the future. Life is change. Stay in the present and observe what is best for your life.

Let me give you an example. When I first started to exercise, a half-mile jog almost killed me! Now I run three miles and enjoy it. Maybe yoga or walking is more suited for your body and life-style. You have to judge how any exercise or diet affects your life and well-being.

I have tried many different ways of eating, from macrobiotic to complete vegetarianism to fasting. My experimentation has led me to the conclusion that no matter how balanced a diet might be, if I don't like it or it doesn't fit my lifestyle, I won't consistently use it. Recently, I needed to find an easier way to eat healthily that I would do consistently. I was in a quandary as to how to get more vegetables into my diet.

When the answers are not obvious, I go within and ask Spirit to guide me because Spirit knows all. When you sincerely ask Spirit from your heart for guidance, answers may come from everyday sources. I recently came to the awareness that I needed more fruits and vegetables in my diet but I personally don't like many vegetables, and this made changing my diet difficult. I was reading about all the research regarding phytonutrients contained in fresh fruits and vegetables and I asked Spirit to help me get them in my body in an easy way. I really specified *easy*. Amazingly, within one week three different people told me about a supplement that was composed only of fruits and vegetables. When I hear a message over and over, especially three times, I try to listen. I tried the supplement, and it has been fantastic for me. (This is how Spirit works. It gives you information through daily life experiences. The more you listen, the more you are guided.) You may find something better suited to you. Just give yourself the permission to know and hear the answers that are right for you. Maybe you will find an answer from a good friend or maybe when you read something an answer will appear. When you have questions regarding your health or diet, know the answers exist and be open to discovering them.

Not taking care of your body is a way of blocking self-love and not being in balance. When you take care of yourself, you send out loving energy. Your friends and family can feel your love vibration when you take positive actions to take care of yourself.

Sickness

When you get sick or cranky you are out of balance. Being out of balance limits your potential for a greater life and for Spirit to flow positively through your life. I know when I don't feel well I am less likely to be kind or giving to anyone because all my energy is being used inwardly to help me get better.

Listen to your body. If you feel tired, rest. Sickness can be caused by many things. Often you get sick simply because your body is telling you it is tired. Sickness can also be a way your body reacts to food that is bad for you. Your body getting sick can be a message that there are emotional issues to address that you have been avoiding.

Most people tell me they don't know what their bodies need. What I usually tell them is to "act as if you know" and the answers will come to you. This is what I mean by becoming more aware. Talk to your body. Ask Spirit to guide you to a person or a solution to help you know what you need to do. Remember, you will always get answers to your questions through Spirit if you ask and then consistently take actions.

If I can come from abusing my health to a place where I am guided and know what I need for my body's balance, so can you. I am not different than anyone else. The answers and help you will receive are contingent on how badly you want to change and how honestly you confront yourself. It is up to you to act on the answers you receive.

The Emotional Body

The emotional self is hard for some people to deal with, because emotions aren't tangible and because most of us have been taught to suppress feelings. Suppressing feelings is a main cause of emotional imbalance.

Emotional balance means an individual has healthy self-esteem and a sense of self-worth. Emotionally balanced people are not afraid to feel their feelings. Most people live life from the neck up, handling life on a strictly intellectual basis.

If you were abused in childhood or come from a dys-functional home, you learned to stuff all those neglected inner child feelings away because then it wasn't safe to feel. It might have been safer for you to handle your life from the intellect alone. Now, you might think if you intellectually understand something, then you don't need to feel the emotion(s) involved in order for you to heal. When you come from this perspective, you limit your healing (and perhaps block it altogether).

Your mind and emotions are distinct, different parts of you as a person, and consequently need distinct and different meth-ods of healing and nurturing. Problems arise when you neglect to give any of your parts the healing and nurturing it needs.

Let me give you an example. In my childhood my emo-tional needs were not met. I suppressed hurt and anger over my childhood for years. The feelings were not gone because I suppressed them — they were just hidden from my conscious mind. Hiding my feelings made me feel worse and limited my effectiveness as a person. Repressing my emotions affected me in concrete, negative ways.

As a child, I understood my mother was sick and she did the best she could for me, but this intellectual understanding didn't help me heal my emotional self. I thought if I understood the situation, I wouldn't feel angry or hurt because my mother couldn't nurture me the way I needed. I tried to bypass emotional healing through intellectual understanding. Because I denied my feelings, I unconsciously created different ways to act out my suppressed feelings of anger and low self-worth. I did this through drinking, drugs, and bulimia.

Many of my clients are amazed to learn they need to experience feelings in order to be truly balanced and in harmony, and they're shocked to learn many problems in their lives are caused by suppressed emotions. They think they are functioning okay when they cut themselves off from any or all of their feelings. But how okay is okay? You can go through life repressing your feelings and survive, but I wanted to be more than a survivor. I wanted to thrive! As I grew in awareness, I knew that for me to be my happiest, most creative self I'd have to heal the emotional part of me. I tell my clients that to heal your feelings you have to feel them, not just "think" them healed. Feeling your feelings is your key to creating a happy, balanced emotional self.

Balancing your emotional part means not only feeling present issues, but also clearing negative emotional issues from your childhood. If your emotions from the past have not been dealt with, you are still living and reacting from them. When you've completely healed the emotional issues from your past, you are able to completely live in the moment. You cannot be in control and create what you want in the present moment if you are reacting from past emotional pain or negative limiting beliefs.

Let me explain. Most of us have discovered some nurturing is missing in our upbringing. This lack of nurturing can create repressed feelings of anger, sadness, and low self-esteem. Maybe you understand your childhood but have never dealt with the hurtful feelings associated with it, consequently you carry around those feelings your entire life. Those emotional energy vibrations are hidden until you become conscious of them, acknowledge them, and feel them. Repressed or denied feelings may manifest as an eating disorder, as I had, or as a drug or alcohol problem. Or, you may have trouble with relationships or accepting love and nurturing from people around you. You might be an over-achiever or overeat consistently using food or accomplishments to fill yourself up emotionally. There can be a multitude of scenarios. Old, unprocessed feelings always affect your decisions and actions, and the quality of your life right now.

For example, a client named Maggie came to me for help with relationships. In seven years, she hadn't accepted more than two dates in a row from any one man because she always found something she didn't like about him. Maggie is not unattractive or disagreeable; she's a gorgeous blond in her late thirties with the nicest personality you could want. As her therapy progressed, I discovered her brother sexually abused her in childhood. Only in the last few years had she let herself be aware of the abuse and then only on an intellectual level. Emotionally she still could not handle the situation. Her repressed emotions intensified her natural tendency to be obsessive and compulsive, a rigid behavior that negates balance and can block emotional healing. One way her obsessive and compulsive behavior manifested was through her eating habits. In the past she had adopted very restrictive and limiting diets, ranging from eating any and all desserts, but only until noon, to eating nothing but beef. As Maggie grew in awareness, she realized her unbalanced ways of eating helped her stay unconscious of what was really bothering her. She realized her obsessive sugar binges kept her feeling physically lightheaded and aggravated a yeast infection she has had for years. Her lightheadedness and yeast condition were ways of staying out of relationships and not confronting the emotional pain caused by her brother's abuse. When she was lightheaded, she didn't have the emotional strength to make good decisions about men or defend her boundaries effectively. When her yeast infection was flaring up, it kept her uninterested in sex and successfully out of long-term relationships. Obsessing about weight or habits are other ways to keep yourself from facing the real, pertinent issues in your own life. The more Maggie obsessed about food and kept her body weak and unbalanced, the less time she had solving her real emotional issues.

Now Maggie is aware that when she eats too much sugar it's because is she wants to be unconscious about something she is feeling. She now understands her unbalanced ways of eating are cues for her growth and larger awareness. Maggie now tries to balance her diet to strengthen her self emotionally, mentally, and physically. She understands more fully how one unbalanced part affects her entire life. Now that she is more loving and nurturing to herself, she is seeing changes in her personality. She has gone from being submissive to being assertive and protective of her boundaries. Instead of seeking out men who are married or emotionally unavailable, Maggie now consciously chooses men who are interested in self-growth and communication.

Maggie's experience is a powerful example of how underlying beliefs or energy are like magnets that attract situations that correspond to your inner beliefs. If you feel angry and worthless, you will attract corresponding situations until you heal your emotional wounds. You are not in control or balanced in the present until you have healed the emotional baggage of your past.

The first step to emotional healing is to acknowledge the emotional side of yourself. Then realize healing is a process that can take time.

Probably, the most important aspect of healing your emotional self is releasing ALL judgments about feelings in general. Many people, including me, were taught that if we cry or show hurt then we are not strong, or if we feel anger we are not good. When you put demeaning judgments on your feelings, it limits or destroys your ability to feel what is necessary for you to heal. Love yourself enough to feel what you need to feel. This allows you to be able to thrive and be completely in the present with your authentic self.

Exercise

Emotional Healing of Your Childhood

This exercise is tremendously powerful. You need to use it over a period of several months. It works whether you remember your childhood or not. Start with ten minutes of chanting your word. This facilitates a feeling of safety and helps you release what you need and receive the good.

Before you start be aware of some aspect of your childhood that you are angry about, such as the loss of a parent, emotional neglect, or feeling lonely. For the sake of healing you are going to face the personification of your anger from your childhood — your parents, siblings, or peers. See them in a dark picture with you standing in front. Give yourself permission to fully express your anger directly to them in your imagination. (This may be hard but let yourself stretch.) Confronting your anger in this way helps you to become free of the past, and expressing it this way is safe and appropriate. Express your anger until you feel or sense some kind of shift. Maybe you will sense lightness around your heart or feel less angry.

Next, imagine reaching inside yourself and pulling out all this dark "goo." The dark "goo" is your unworthiness, powerlessness, victimhood and shame. Give it to the symbolic part in your picture. Next, emphatically tell the people in the picture, "I am taking back my power to be happy, healthy, and confident." See your power as a bright light. Reach inside them and take your power back. Put it in your heart and stomach.

Next, look around for a golden sword, and pick it up. Notice a dark umbilical cord of energy connecting you and those in the picture. Take a deep breath and cut the cord. See them dissolve. Immediately turn in the opposite direction and connect with a

> *bright, happy picture of you in a happy new child-*
> *hood (or happy adulthood). You may need to do*
> *this many times, but it is extremely worth it.*〜

As you work on your emotional healing, you might want to seek professional counseling. Give yourself permission to do whatever it takes to claim your emotional self without shame or fear. Not having a fully functioning emotional self is a handicap; you function and get around, but not as freely as you could if you didn't have the handicap. Be all you can be and learn to love your emotional self. After all, God gave you emotions for a reason.

The Mental Body

Your mental self or body comprises both the conscious mind and the unconscious mind. The conscious mind is the seat of reason and logic. The unconscious mind holds all your habits and deeper beliefs.

Achieving mental balance takes cooperation and understanding. When your mind is in harmony, your conscious and unconscious minds work toward the same objective, and your thoughts produce peace and tranquility. When the two aspects of your mind are in conflict, you have trouble reaching your objectives.

Let's say you want to quit smoking. The logical, conscious mind realizes smoking is bad for your health. So you decide to quit, but part of you gets in the way. You keep hearing little messages from your unconscious mind, like "Smoking is my friend," or "It will be too tough to live without cigarettes." Those goal-blocking messages come from your unconscious mind, which has no logic or reason. Your thought process is divided because your conscious mind thinks one way and your unconscious mind another.

To achieve mental harmony, both parts of your mind have to believe the same thing. Because the unconscious mind has no logic or reason, it keeps the old beliefs until you find a way to change them. The unconscious mind is the more powerful of the two, and even if you want to consciously change, first you must change any unconscious beliefs that are in conflict with your conscious desire. The unconscious mind runs like a computer — it doesn't analyze information, it just performs. To achieve your objectives, you first have to discover what belief(s) your unconscious mind is holding that are blocking your progress.

How can you do this? I tell my clients to look at what is in their lives right now. For example, if you consciously believe you want to be thinner and you have been overweight for a length of time, unconsciously for some reason you feel more comfortable being heavy. This holds true with everything in your life. Whatever is presently in your life represents the true beliefs you hold, whether they involve money, relationships, health, or anything else.

Positive Thinking

One way to change your unconscious thought processes is to use positive thinking. To do this, consciously monitor the thoughts you create, and if they are negative or in conflict with your goals, change them. Only you create your thoughts so become a master of what you allow yourself to think. The mind needs gentle awareness, not a firm hand. When you find yourself off track, gently put your consciousness back on your goal in that very moment. Consistency is vital for success!

I have discovered mental programming will only take you so far in changing thought patterns. Eventually, you have to go above the mind to correct erroneous thinking and tap into your spiritual self. Remember that the mind, emotions, and body are tools used by Soul to live in this dimension. Soul is in control. The mind is limited by its physical nature so there are limits to its growth and power.

I use positive thinking and affirmations, but I also get in touch with my spiritual self every day and open myself up to God and myself as Soul. That way, I know all my thoughts are being affected in a profound and powerful way for my highest good and the good of all. Contemplations (ways of getting connected to Spirit) definitely help balance your mind in the best direction for your highest purpose. And when you live your life based on the Holy Spirit, your lower bodies (your mind, emotions, and physical body) are balanced and affected in the best way possible. When you know what part of you is out of balance, it is easier to bring your whole life into harmony.

Actions That Create Balance

Each of your bodies affects the other parts of yourself, your outlook on life, and the actions you take. If one part of your life overshadows another, imbalance occurs. If you work all the time and don't take time to rest or play, you eventually become unbalanced. This lessens your effectiveness as a person.

To drive home this point, I want to share with you the realizations of Dr. Cindi. Dr. Cindi came to me at her wits' end. She was feeling out of control and exhausted. At her first session she told me she had barely eked out the hour to see me.

During our first session, I found out she never gave herself any free time or did anything to nurture herself. She gave all her time and energy to her patients, husband, and children. She was a typical dysfunctional nurturer, accepting all the responsibility of her business and home life, leaving no time for herself. Dr. Cindi wanted peace of mind badly, and she was willing to embrace new concepts. I explained to her about balance and self-love. I told her when she took time out to recharge and have fun her whole life would prosper. I emphasized the need for healthy boundaries and releasing the responsibility for other adults. I then put her through the hypnosis process to bring these new concepts deeper into her unconscious.

She came back the next week beaming! During the space of a week, she set boundaries with her teenage son and husband and scheduled two half-days off to have fun. She felt like a new woman. Before, she couldn't even see how she was going to come for an hour's session; now, because her conscious and unconscious beliefs were coming into harmony, she was aware she could change anything in her life. Week after week, her life continued to improve. Her business increased as well as her time off. Her good family relationships got even better, and she noticed how her energy affected everyone in her life. When she felt balanced and nurtured, she could see more patients and have a deeper, more satisfying family life. She realized her energy affected everything in her life, and when she was out of balance, so was the rest of her life. Before she was a victim; now she is on the road to mastery!

Balance occurs and is created in the moment. There are times when it is right and balanced to work more, and there are times when it is perfect to play more. I always ask myself this question to discover what I need for my own balance and harmony: **"What do I need at this moment to create value in my life now?"**

This question helps me zero in on what I need for balance and harmony. Value to me means allowing me to be all I can be in every category of my life. In the higher regard, value also means anything that helps me open to my spiritual self as Soul. So when I ask myself this question, I am as honest as I can be about my progress.

When I ask myself what I need to create value in my life now, it helps me focus on my responsibility for my own happiness and well-being. This question helps to put me in the driver's seat to take actions to create my happiness. When I am happy, it affects others in a positive way because my energy and vibrations are more positive. Creating value for myself helps me to stop relating to others in unhealthy ways, because I know it is up to me and no one else to make my own balance and happiness.

Let's say I've been working very hard, and I feel burned out and unproductive. I may feel tired and drained because my emotional self needs fun or my physical body needs a rest, or a combination of both. I may not know what I need right away, but if I continue to work hard and stay unbalanced, something is going to suffer. I have to take responsibility to find out what I need right now to create balance in my life, and then allow myself to get what I need.

If you don't know what you need, try different actions until something clicks. Actions, actions, actions are always the key to change and accomplishments. Without actions, you stay powerless and a victim. Actions place you more in being the master of your life! You will find out more quickly what you need in your life, whether it is rest, play, more work, communication, or nurturing, by the daily action of connecting to your spiritual nature.

When I am not sure what I need for my greatest good, I go within myself and ask. You will be surprised at how much you really know about what you need when you ask yourself. Allowing yourself to know is the beginning of self-awakening.

I am amazed when people say they don't know what they need or want in life. If you really don't know, act as if you do.

Eventually, you will allow yourself to know. As Soul, you always know the answers. These answers go beyond logic and reason to pure understanding.

Next, let yourself have what you need. This is usually hard to do. You probably have been taught to deny your needs. You may believe your needs are not important or that you will be a better person if you let others' needs take precedence over yours. Whenever you deny your own growth or needs you will suffer, and so will everyone around you. When you deny your needs, you deny parts of yourself. Remember that neglecting any one of your parts is the same as neglecting your whole self; you then live incompletely. This diminishes the positive effects on yourself and everyone else.

Mothers usually have a really hard time meeting their needs because they have been programmed to fill everyone's needs before their own. Over time, they can become unbalanced, as Dr. Cindi found out. They neglect their spiritual, emotional, mental, or physical selves and wonder why they feel depressed or are overweight or sick. Moms who are depressed, sick, or feeling bad about their bodies affect the whole family. The same is true with fathers. Many fathers work too hard and neglect themselves. They then have nothing left to give themselves, their wives, or their children.

Try to touch base with your inner self a little more often. Give yourself permission to have what you need, whether it's fun or time to rest. You will become balanced, more capable, and a much happier person.

Allowing yourself permission to have what you need is important. Without it, you create a life that doesn't allow balance. You have to give balance to yourself. It doesn't magically appear.

I have had a hard time giving myself permission to have fun or to take time off. Until recently, I worked six or seven days a week. I found myself living a one-dimensional existence. There was a part of me that felt if I didn't work all the time, I wouldn't survive. But I kept asking Spirit to guide me in my growth and to help me manifest my creativity. Circumstances kept presenting themselves in such a way that I had to take more time off. Through this forced time away from work, I realized how important time away was for my health and emotional well-being. I now incorporate more time off in my schedule. I make as much income as before, but I am happier and I have time for my creative endeavors, which include painting and writing, as well as my physical sports and exercise.

Balance in life and within your separate bodies is very individual. Someone may need five hours of sleep and do fine, while you may need ten. You may need to play more than your spouse, or you may need more quiet time than anyone you know. Know whatever you need in the present moment to create value in your whole being is okay. Do whatever you need to do to grow toward self-mastery and true happiness. This is what a balanced, whole life is all about: your personal journey to your true self. Give yourself permission to take the steps you need for this journey, including creating balance and harmony in all aspects of yourself and your daily life.

The more you ask yourself for balance, the more you will know how to create it and live it!

CHAPTER EIGHT

Anger

Volcanic energy
hidden from self.
Excess baggage
timed to explode.
Anytime, anywhere.
In the most unexpected ways.

Children, we're so afraid
to feel,
to acknowledge,
this pent up rage.

Why do you stuff it inside
thinking it's not there;
only it is.
Eating away at your life,
your joy,
your health.

Bring it up and out,
acknowledge it.
Free yourself
from those invisible chains.
Not to harm another,
but to create value
for yourself.
Make a place now
In your life
for love.

P art of your growth as Soul is learning to create value with anger, then transcending the need for it. As much as you may try, you can never transcend anger until you acknowledge it, learn how to constructively release it in the moment, and experience and release in an appropriate manner, anger you may have repressed from your past. Until you learn how to create value with your anger, it will continuously affect your life in negative ways.

How is anger affecting your life? If you ask this question and allow yourself to be honest, your answers will emerge. This chapter will help you to identify, process, and understand anger more completely. I think most people are shocked to hear anger can create value at all. After reading this chapter, I hope you will see your anger in a new light and see that you can experience and release it in new ways that will create value for you.

Anger as Energy

Understanding what anger is helps you deal with it more effectively. Anger is energy. As you know, all we are composed of energy. Since energy comes in different shapes and forms, everything you think of as "you" is energy, including your thoughts, emotions, and physical body.

When you realize anger is very real, as real as physical objects, you are then on your way to greater growth and change, broadening your view of what is real. When you make this shift regarding anger, you can use this awareness to evolve in your personal and spiritual life and you can take more effective actions.

Maybe you have learned to suppress your anger, or maybe you rage on others. Suppressing your anger ends up hurting you and rage hurts others. Therefore, what other options are there to deal with your anger?

In the life path of growth, it is important to neither suppress anger or rage on others. There are healthy ways to deal with anger, such as acknowledging your anger in the present moment and healing old anger you repressed. Throughout this chapter I will give you effective tools to create value through your anger — past or present.

Creating value means doing what is best for your own growth or development as a human and a spiritual being without infringing on others' boundaries. To others, it may not always appear you're creating value, and that's okay. To truly grow, it is important to do what you feel is right for your life and spiritual self in the present moment as long as you respect the boundaries of others. Only you know what is right for you, and as an individual you need different experiences for your personal and spiritual development.

Defending Your Boundaries

Creating value may mean dealing with your anger in ways others don't always agree with. Others may not like the way you handle a situation or express yourself even if the communication is respectful. Respectful communication comprises communicating your boundaries without demeaning others. When you communicate your anger with respect, you open the door for love and growth and create value. For example, in my life I've had a very hard time accepting my anger and expressing it, especially to my family or to people who are close to me. I found it especially hard to tell one of my sisters that she irritated me sometimes. The issues were usually about my boundaries as a person, and sometimes I got angry when I felt she invalidated my feelings.

In my past, I repressed my feelings and I wouldn't say what bothered me. I even hid my anger from my conscious self. When I handled my anger this way, I felt like a victim and my self-worth suffered — I was cutting myself off from self-love when I didn't stand up for myself. My sister didn't realize she was upsetting me. Most people don't know they are stepping on your toes, your boundaries, until you tell them. If you don't tell others what is bothering you, who will? Realize people live life from their own set of boundaries and rules. It is natural that people will have different boundaries. This doesn't make them bad, just different.

Step by step, I started voicing my anger when I felt my feelings or personal boundaries were invalidated. I learned how to have a respectful tone in my voice and to speak calmly even when I was upset. I used my energy and my personal power to stand up for myself without losing respect for others or myself. When I first stood up to my sister, she criticized me for expressing anger, but I kept defending my emotional boundaries, learning how to be respectful while expressing my needs. Since I started standing up for myself, I have a better relationship with my sister, and I have better self-esteem and feelings of self-worth.

This is just one example of how acknowledging my anger created value, simply because I communicated my boundaries in appropriate and respectful ways for both myself and the other party. The very act of protecting yourself and your feelings is an act of self-love because you are refusing to be abused in any way. This is a powerful, internal way to increase your self-worth.

Communicating your anger can be a tremendous growth step. Expressing your feelings is acknowledging another part of yourself; this is, in essence, living your authentic self. When you communicate your anger to others with the intention to release barriers to love, they have the chance to be their authentic selves with you. Repressed anger prevents the flow of love to yourself or to others. People may or may not be ready to handle this deeper, more real way of communicating. But, if you never give yourself the chance to be genuine with others, you could miss opportunities with many people who are ready for this deeper relationship.

People will not always understand your internal needs or struggles, and they don't need to understand them. What is important is that you understand what you need and work on what is right for you. This creates value for your life. It's also important that you do not take away anyone else's rights while you are standing up for your own. Most people feel angry when they feel their boundaries have been ignored or violated. Defending your boundaries as an individual is not infringing on another person or an act of aggression. It is protecting yourself from someone else's aggression or ignorance of what your wants or needs are.

Beliefs About Anger

Your beliefs about anger and how to express it were formed in your childhood. The more you know about how your beliefs were formed, the more comprehensively you can help yourself change. In my family, we learned indirectly and through the direct actions of my parents that we were not allowed to openly express anger, and that angry people were bad. This affected the quality of my relationships with my friends and how I felt about myself. Every time I felt angry, I internalized the feeling of being worthless, when in reality I was being human! When I became conscious of this past conditioning, I gained some power to change my negative feelings about myself when I became angry.

You may also carry strong beliefs about anger from previous lives, but since most of us don't remember our past lives, it's best to deal with anger in the present moment. Even if you are manifesting anger from a previous life, you can only grow and change in this present moment.

If you come from some kind of dysfunctional home, your upbringing may generate a tremendous amount of anger. Sometimes you are aware of it, but most often you are not. Many of my clients have great compassion and intellectual understanding about their parents and their upbringing. They realize their parents did the best job they could. They can mentally understand, "my parents were alcoholics," or "there was sickness," or "my parents had bad childhoods too."

Many people think that understanding why their parents weren't able to give them the nurturing they needed makes everything all right. They think their intellectual understanding should override feelings of anger. My clients are very surprised to learn they need to feel their anger before they can thoroughly heal or release it.

Thinking you can heal an emotional hurt with only conscious, intellectual understanding is like saying, "My body shouldn't hurt after running a marathon because I know how to run." Or it's like a doctor saying, "She shouldn't get sick because her knowledge of the body will stave off sickness."

I have discovered most of us don't know how to feel and heal our emotional selves. I cannot emphasize this enough: You cannot heal your emotional self with mental understanding alone! To fully heal an emotional trauma (past or present), you have to experience your feelings regarding that trauma and not deny that they exist. Many people have had traumas from their childhood. Conscious feeling and acknowledgment of repressed emotions is what your emotional body needs for healing.

Your inner emotional self can be scared to death to experience anger you feel toward your mom or dad or whomever was your primary caretaker. Your inner emotional self may feel that if you become angry toward your parents, they won't love you or take care of you, and you won't survive. (Many of us also accept the mass societal belief that you are a shameful person if you are angry with your parents for any reason.)

If you don't consciously understand your inner negative beliefs regarding anger ahead of time, acknowledging this anger can make you feel unworthy and fill you with guilt. To protect yourself from feeling unworthy, you learn to repress your feelings of anger or project your anger onto others or into unhealthy ways of living. Consequently, you never learn to take care of anger honestly in ways that benefit your total growth.

The message being played out in your unconscious mind could sound something like this, "After all, my parents brought me into this world and I owe them my life and gratitude," or "These people did the best they could and I shouldn't feel angry." The unconscious messages that keep playing in your head negatively affect everything in your life because they are your fundamental beliefs. They limit you and keep you from being free.

As babies and young children, you have a limitless need for nurturing and attention. Even if there was such a thing as a perfect childhood, I believe a child would have some anger over not getting enough of what he or she perceived was needed. Anger over your childhood, therefore, is quite normal, and this anger is intensified when there is dysfunction in the home.

If you came from a home where the caretakers were not nurtured as children, they probably didn't have the emotional capacity to give you all the love and nurturing you needed. Children learn from the people around them. If the primary caretakers love themselves, their children incorporate their healthy self-esteem. The same is true if the caretakers lack nurturing in their lives now. This lack of nurturing is mirrored to children, who absorb it and feel they created it. Children interpret any lack as something intrinsically wrong with them.

This is what happened to me. Because of her illness, my mother could not emotionally nurture me enough. Usually, in this case, the child ends up nurturing the parent and repressing the anger. That's exactly what I did. I repressed my anger and it manifested through my bulimia and drug use. Anger is a natural and normal response for not getting what you needed as a child. If I had felt safe to feel and openly express my anger appropriately when I was a child, I believe my bulimia and drug abuse would not have occurred. I could have released my anger energy from my life in the moment, instead of projecting it in the distorted ways I did.

Repressed Anger

Repressing any emotion or dealing with emotions in unhealthy ways keeps you from growing personally and spiritually. Your anger energy is not being expressed constructively when you repress it. This prevents love and acceptance from shining through you as a whole person. Anger, repressed or when you rage, keeps you from self-love. Without total self-love, it is impossible to really love anyone else fully or to fully develop your self in any way. When you deal with your feelings in the moment and acknowledge what you're feeling, you can release unwanted feelings more quickly and live completely in the present with a deeper ability to love.

It is important to identify your anger and learn how to deal with it constructively. Remember, everything about you is energy, and it can change forms. Repressed anger can show up in physical, mental, or emotional ways.

Chronic sickness or disease can be an effect of long-term repressed emotions...like anger. For example, eczema, hypertension, and ulcers can be caused by or exacerbated by repressed stress. Most of us accept this, and the medical profession believes this to be true. Take this principle further. Entertain the concept that all emotions affect the body in some way, good and bad.

If you have a disease or are constantly getting sick, take stock of past and present events. See if you have angry feelings you have been afraid to feel or acknowledge. As a child, I was always sick. When I started to express my feelings in my teen years, my health improved tremendously.

Another sign of repressed anger is depression. Energy has to go somewhere, even if you have been consciously denying it. If anger is still there, you might experience it as depression. Most depression is anger energy turned inward. Anger kept inside can be destructive emotionally, mentally, and physically.

Being sick and depressed are less than satisfactory ways to live, and even if you are not interested in living a more spiritual life, you can benefit from releasing denied anger. If you want to reach higher spiritual heights, releasing pent-up anger is absolutely necessary! Whenever you are repressing anger, you are directly causing destruction to yourself, and indirectly affecting others as well.

Spirit needs a clear vehicle to flow through. The more you become conscious of your hidden anger, the sooner you can process it in healthy ways and begin to love yourself more completely. You can then open your life more fully to be a channel for Spirit and God.

Another sign of repressed anger is self-sabotage. This is hard to recognize because self-sabotage takes on so many forms. When you keep making choices that keep you from happiness or reaching your goals, they are signs of self-sabotage. Most of the time, you aren't consciously feeling the anger responsible for your behavior.

If any of these things have happened to you over and over again or in any combination, odds are you are repressing anger. Things might seem to "just happen" to you. You keep meeting the wrong kinds of people, and the relationships you develop are destructive or ineffectual or you get sick all the time. Maybe you rationalize how all the jobs you've had never worked out.

Maybe you never finish the projects you start, whether these are school, hobby, or work related. Other self-sabotage actions are detrimental habits like overeating, drugs, alcohol, cigarette smoking, exercise to the point of obsession or bodily injury, frequent accidents, and lack of motivation. These are common (but definitely not all) ways you can sabotage yourself. The list goes on and on.

If these scenarios sound familiar and you've tried to change them without results, you are probably angry at something or someone (which could include yourself). Some issue — maybe more than one — in your life is not being dealt with directly.

When you deal with anger in these ways you probably were taught, directly or indirectly, that expressing anger was bad. You may have been punished for feeling anger or showing it. Consequently, instead of dealing with anger directly, you deal with anger unconsciously. Let me give you an example. My bulimia was one of many ways I sabotaged my own life, and it came partly from my repressed anger. In my heart, I was furious at my mother for being sick. I was angry I didn't get the nurturing, love, and attention a child needs. I was never aware of this consciously while I was growing up. My bulimia was an outer manifestation of my internal rage.

We were taught never to show anger, but my anger energy was still there. This energy had to manifest somehow. My unconscious mind picked bulimia to vent my hidden rage because I couldn't deal with it directly. This way of dealing with my anger was definitely hurting my body and the quality of my life. My bulimia started to go away when I consciously worked on developing my self-worth and confronting my anger.

The more I confront myself and all my hidden emotional issues or beliefs, the more I grow spiritually and the more harmonious my daily life becomes. In my past, I was terrified to face my anger directly. As a teenager and young adult I would virtually shake from head to toe when I had to tell someone I didn't like something or that I was, heaven forbid, angry at them. Instinctively, I knew I had to challenge myself to confront people and issues that bothered me, or I would remain a bulimic and emotionally numb for the rest of my life. It took me fourteen years to overcome my bulimia, but I did overcome it!

Everyone at one time or another represses anger. Even if you're the kind of person who beats up on people and is openly nasty and critical, what's behind your actions is your hidden anger. People who are openly violent have short fuses because they have not resolved their anger which is usually from their childhoods. Even when they beat up on people, the aggression and rage do not help them confront and heal their real emotional wounds. They are reacting instead of healing, and they are probably terrified of actually feeling all the anger from the past.

Many people unconsciously believe if they feel all their feelings they will physically die. No one ever dies from experiencing feelings, but many people are killing themselves with all the feelings they repress. People are scared to feel, just the same.

So what do you do with your repressed anger? How do you heal it? How can you be human, deal with your anger, and grow spiritually, all at the same time?

Acknowledging Repressed Anger

The first step in the process of dealing with anger is to realize and acknowledge you are angry. If you cannot acknowledge what you need in order to change, you may never make headway with your growth. The next step is to know that no one is perfect. Anger is only an emotion. Let go of all judgments about what it means. When you let go of judgments about anger, this frees you up to feel it. Feeling your anger is the only way to process it. Releasing judgments about your feelings is paramount to your growth and healing. **A feeling is just a feeling. It is neither good nor bad, it just is. It's what you do with it that creates value or not.**

In your spiritual and personal growth, it can be very powerful to believe whatever is happening to you is perfect. At first this may be hard to understand. When you deeply understand that whatever is in your life is the next step in your evolution as Soul, you can drop all judgments and use what is happening in a detached, constructive way for your growth. Over the course of your life, this attitude will help you recognize man-made rules or beliefs that prevent you from embracing your spiritual evolution. All of your experiences and feelings are teaching you something important on your road to God.

As Soul, you always have free will. You can choose to stay a victim, or you can grow. At any moment in time you are either creating what you want or being a victim. There is no in-between. You have to accept and take control of your life if you want to grow, no matter what has happened in the past or what is happening now.

It's one thing to understand and process your emotions about your childhood, and it is quite another to languish in blame about your past. People who sincerely want to evolve tackle the past and learn from it. They do any and all emotional work necessary to heal.

To completely heal, you must release blame and anger about your past. Blaming or staying angry is remaining a victim. Taking action to change yourself is being the master of your life. When you understand your life from the highest perspective as Soul, you realize your life experiences, from childhood on, were either effects from past karma or results of present-day choices. So who can you really blame?

Stages of Loss

Suppose you've realized you have repressed anger. Consciously you have decided to deal with your feelings so you can further grow in Spirit. Your next step is going through the stages of loss.

Simply put, the stages of loss are denial, anger, hurt, and resolution. Denial is the act of not consciously admitting to a feeling or an understanding about a particular event. After confronting the situation, the next phase a person goes through is anger. Next come feelings of hurt and sadness. A person can go in and out of denial while experiencing anger and hurt. (The process is a flow, not a rigid schedule.) All feelings have to be acknowledged and experienced fully to be resolved. When you reach resolution about something you have been angry about, you have released anger on every level. You can then be fully in the present.

A former client of mine named George illustrates this point clearly. George is a middle-aged man who was having trouble keeping jobs, even jobs that were below his potential. He had been feeling depressed and had lacked motivation for several years. I found out that several years earlier he had an important corporate job, and he had been fired unfairly. His lack of motivation and job spiral corresponded to his firing. I deduced he was repressing anger toward that past situation, and his internal anger energy was manifesting as self-sabotage. I explained my theory to George. He understood, and he started the emotional work of going through the stages of loss regarding his former job. Learning how repressed emotions were hurting his present life brought him out of denial about being fired. We next worked on his anger and sadness regarding his loss. After all the emotions were processed, he came to resolution regarding his situation. George realized he was still a worthy individual whether he got fired or not. Eventually he gained more confidence and motivation and landed a job on par with his skills and expertise.

This is a very real situation where repressed emotions (in this case, mostly anger) kept George from living fully in the moment. He was still carrying around anger about being fired — anger that kept him from having a full life. Whenever you experience loss of any kind, you have to go through emotional release to heal. The time frame for each loss can vary from minutes to years. The more conscious you are of your repressed emotions, the more quickly you can heal.

Exercise

Processing Anger Appropriately

These exercises can be used whenever you have anger, repressed or not. You can use the ones that follow or come up with your own. You are Soul, and you know what you need. Give yourself permission to know.

1. The Anger Letter — Write a letter and express your full-fledged anger to the person or situation about which you are angry. Do not hold back or make it an intellectual experience. Express from your "gut" exactly how angry you feel. Don't get caught in the trap of rationalizing away your anger feelings. Write down all the trapped feelings of anger, and then either burn the letter or rip it up. Under no circumstances do you give it to any person. This is for your release only. You may need to do this more than once, and this is okay.

2. A spiritual exercise — Start by singing a high vibratory word for about ten minutes. Sit in a comfortable position. Mentally state that you want to release your anger so you can grow as Soul and have more Divine Love in your life. With this attitude, you are letting go of negative karma, and the results will be for your highest good. Next, see or feel your anger as darkness or as a heaviness leaving your heart each time you exhale. Do this for as long as you need to. You may notice a shift of some kind, maybe lightness in your heart area or warmth that was not there before. When you notice some kind of shift, imagine the Light of God coming into your heart. With every intake of breath say to yourself, "I am worthy of this Love," and "I am safe to receive this Love." Breathe slowly and deeply. Do this for several minutes.

3. A contemplation — Imagine a beautiful nature setting. It is spring, the sun is shining, and the birds are singing. You are totally safe and in awe of the beauty. You come to a waterfall. It is sparkling light. You go over to it and take off your shoes. There is a path under the light and you go stand under the stream of light with your arms outstretched. You mentally ask Spirit to wash away all the anger and negativity within you with the healing energy of the light. As it flows over you, look down at your feet and see all this dark "goo" leaving your body. The dark "goo" is your conscious and unconscious negative energy that has been inside your mind, body, or emotions. At the same time, you receive the Divine Love that is the light.

4. A more basic physical exercise — Find a quiet place in your house and some pillows. Either hit the pillows with your fists or place a pillow over your mouth and scream into it. Anger is energy that needs to be released from your body. Sometimes you just have to move your body to accomplish this. ∽

Shifting Your Consciousness

You can use many scenarios in contemplation. The important thing to remember is to get your vibrations higher and more tuned into Spirit. You do this by singing a high-vibratory word until you sense a shift in your state of consciousness. The shift can be very subtle. A shift in awareness tunes your vibrations to a higher level. It can be reframing of your thought patterns to the higher purpose of life, or it can be the subtle feeling of being protected and connected more strongly to your spiritual heritage. You may hear Sound and see Light in your contemplations or observe very subtle changes in the way you look at life. Just singing a high-vibratory word creates a shift in your inner self whether you are aware of it or not. If you can't feel a shift, sing the word of

your choice for about ten to twenty minutes anyway, then do
your contemplations. Even if you don't feel anything, do the
contemplations consistently. With repetition you will come to
know when shifts occur in your consciousness.

Allowing the Process of Change

Keep in mind that change is a process. The more consistently you work on ridding yourself of old stuff, the more
success you will have. You may need to do all of these exercises and more. You may need professional counseling to help
you sort out your anger.

Keep working with it, and your life will change. The
actions you take create effects, even if you can't see the results
right away. The results will manifest if you are sincere and consistent in wanting to evolve as Soul.

The more you consciously work with Spirit for your
growth, the more you will recognize everything is part of
Spirit. You will become more aware that the right tools and
solutions are being sent to you all the time. The more you listen for the answers with all of your being, the faster you grow
and solve your problems. There is no problem in your life
without a solution.

Reasons We Keep Anger

There are four major reasons you may hold on to anger.
1. You want to punish yourself or someone else.
2. You want to hold on to a person or situation.
3. You want to avoid working on your own issues.
4. You have used anger to survive in some way.

Keep this list handy. When you have anger and are having a
hard time releasing it, read this list honestly. You will likely find
that one or several of the reasons hold true.

Let's look at them one by one.

1. You want to punish yourself or someone else.

Has someone "done you wrong?" You have probably mulled over and over in your mind the horrible way someone treated you, and you want to punish that person. Or maybe you have made some kind of mistake or done something you perceived as "bad," and you won't forgive yourself and go on with your life. You instead hold on to anger and end up hurting yourself with self-sabotaging behaviors, feeling depressed, or maybe you may project the anger you feel about yourself onto someone else. Remember anger is either repressed or externalized.

2. You want to hold on to a person or situation.

You may be unconscious of your desire to hold on to a person or situation, like when you have a romantic breakup. You may have been the one who initiated the breakup, but your anger is still evident. The emotional part of you is taking more time to release the relationship than your conscious mind. Or perhaps you had a horribly unhappy childhood. Your conscious mind says, "My past is past and it no longer affects me," but you notice that when you talk or think about the past you are still angry about it. This indicates that an emotional part of you wants to hang on to the past by staying angry. This is because emotionally you want a different version, a better version to have happened. Therefore, you are not over your past until you feel emotionally neutral.

3. You want to avoid working on your own issues.

By staying angry toward someone or something, you keep yourself from true responsibility. Focusing on the "other" can be a wonderful illusion for your ego. They have to change but you don't. True responsibility means living your life from a higher perspective. Even if someone has done you wrong, take a look at your thinking, emotions, or physical actions to see what lessons you need for your higher spiritual growth.

4. You have used anger to survive in some way.

This may be more difficult to pinpoint, but by consistently observing your behavior you can spot this pattern. Maybe from childhood you learned that when you were angry you could function better or you felt safer in some way. This behavior pattern stays with you because you are getting some of your basic needs met. This plays out in adulthood not as healthy, respectful communication of your boundaries, but as something more like a nuclear attack on another person when you feel wronged.

Now you have a checklist of why you keep anger. How do you go about releasing it? Using all the exercises in this chapter and the following affirmations directed at each reason can facilitate even more release. Write these each day filling in the blanks were needed, and observe your behavior and feelings.

I am now releasing the need to punish_____.

I am safe to let go of_____.

I am becoming more and more conscious of what I need to learn regarding_____.

I no longer need anger to survive.

I communicate my boundaries in healthy, respectful ways.

I replace my anger with Divine Love.

These are just a few to get you started. Look at your life and situation and create your own affirmations. They are always more powerful if you write them each day. Figure out the reasons you hold onto anger, and then create affirmations in the present tense to counter your beliefs that keep the anger in place.

Several factors keep anger trapped. One big, big reason many people can't get rid of anger is because of the ego. When you base your life from the ego, your smaller self, it is easy to feel righteous and justified in keeping anger. Experiencing anger to create value or to protect your boundaries comes from an attitude and intention of love and growth, as opposed to expressing anger from the ego or punishing other people for their points of view. There is a vast difference between the two.

Humans experience anger. It's what you do with it that makes all the difference in your growth. Your ego is always struggling to be heard. When you live from your ego, you stay caught in turmoil and situations that keep you at a lower vibration.

The way to higher growth is to always remember whatever is happening to you is perfect. Your life is unfolding exactly as it should to develop your spiritual self. You can choose to look at any situation as garbage or as Spirit trying to teach you, guiding you more and more toward Divine Love. You can hold on to anger for your petty ego's sake, or you can see what you can learn from the situation. The choice is yours.

Emotional survival is another huge reason we hold on to anger. As a child perhaps you learned to survive by keeping anger. It may not be beneficial to your life now or manifest in logical ways, but your emotional self is not logical. Here is an exercise to help you confront and transform your anger part.

Exercise

Transforming Your Anger Part

Imagine yourself surrounded by spiritual white Light. You are in a very safe beautiful place. It can be either indoors or outdoors. Go up to the part of you that is angry. Imagine what it looks like. See its shape and color. Notice its size. Feel how you feel when you confront this part of yourself. Remember the Light surrounds you and you are safe. Next, communicate to this part your appreciation for all the work it has done for you. Intellectually you may resist this, but remember that, on some level, this part of you has helped you survive some aspect of your life.

Send your appreciation from your heart, not your head. You are thanking your anger part for its intention, not how it acts out. When you truly come from your heart you will notice a shift in the way this part looks to you or how you feel. It may have gotten smaller, changed colors, or moved. Take this as a sign that your appreciation has gotten through. Now ask the part to take on a larger job, one that will help you to thrive, not just survive. Sense if it is willing to accept this. When it does, take this part to a beautiful pond filled with sparkling light. Both of you get in. Breathe in the light. Now give your anger part a new job — one of self-love, healthy boundaries, and forgiveness instead of inappropriate anger. Focus on the Light. When you sense inner acceptance, you have made a concrete change. Next, both of you step out of the pond and notice how the part looks now. ⌒

Anger Keeps You Connected

When you stay at a consistent vibration of anger, you release control of your life to the people or things that make you angry. Your anger keeps you tied to anything it is focused on. Instead of attaining freedom, you get imprisoned with your anger. You may feel independent of your parents, other people, or situations when actually you are emotionally tied to them through anger. You need to go through the stages of loss to break free from their control. Anger is necessary to break through a loss; not getting what you need is definitely a loss.

But you then need to move on. Experience the sadness and hurt you feel after the anger comes up, then resolve the situation or come to completion with whomever or whatever you had been angry about. If you don't finish the stages of loss, you are using energy to hold the loss in your life and you have reduced your freedom to grow.

Another example of holding on to anger occurs in a romantic relationship where one person wants out before the other does. When someone you care about very much has broken up with you, staying angry with the person keeps you connected emotionally. You may not always realize this is what you are doing. Anger is always a very strong emotional link. You keep the anger about the break-up because unconsciously you are afraid to release the relationship even though you've lost the other person's love.

The Time Frame for Releasing Anger

Coming to terms emotionally and spiritually with anger can be tricky. Your anger may have many layers. Work at releasing it until you feel at peace. Some situations will need only a little of your time and effort to change; others may take longer. It's taken me years of effort and different methods to release anger from my childhood, but I believe I finally have. I am freer than I have ever been in my life. For the first time, I am creating my life the way I want it to be. I am no longer carrying around huge, painful chunks of my past. Releasing repressed anger is definitely worth the work!

Until you heal all repressed anger, you are a puppet on a string, bandied about by an internal vision of what you think is true, but what you think is true is just an old movie. Do you want to be led by the past or do you want to take command of your life? Your future is being created by your actions now. What are you creating?

You need to address your anger to come to the realization, on all levels, that there is only Divine Love. You cannot have Divine Love in your life or become Divine Love in the spiritual sense without dealing with all your anger. Be honest with yourself about anger. It is teaching you something. Most often, it teaches you about the Divine Love of God. If every time you got angry you asked, "What is my anger trying to teach me?," you could grow faster. Acknowledge all your anger. It is helping you grow toward Divine Love!

CHAPTER NINE

Guilt and Fear

Trapped in the passages
of time,
they lay hidden,
festering and black.
Body and mind
unable to heal,
what insidious
creations.
Death to all growth
and love.
We are our own
captives.
We are our own
prisoners.
Only we have the key
to freedom.
Only we can pardon
ourselves!

Guilt and fear hamper your growth as an individual in every way — physically, emotionally, creatively, and spiritually. You can live without guilt and fear in your life or at least greatly reduce their effects and power. The less you live your life based on guilt and fear, the stronger, happier, and more loving you can be. Remember, you always have choices. You can have a life dictated by uplifting, conscious beliefs and actions, or a life hampered by unconscious, limiting emotions. The choice is always yours. If you want to eliminate or reduce the hold these negating emotions have over you, please read on.

Guilt

Guilt and its stronger counterpart, shame, are developed in childhood. Guilt, in essence, is the feeling you get when you perceive you have done something wrong. Shame is feeling in the depths of your being that you are the mistake or unworthy. Guilt and shame are learned through the interaction of the modeling you received from the time you were born to the time you were able to reason. Most psychologists agree that reasoning ability is fully formed by the age of ten.

During the time you are developing your reasoning ability, you are the most unconsciously suggestive. You learn very directly, and all the information is taken very quickly and deeply into your unconscious mind. From birth until age three or four you have few personal or mental boundaries as an individual. You deeply absorb all that happens from your interactions with others. You don't have full conscious understanding that most of what you are learning is someone else's behavior or beliefs and not yours. At this time, it is hard for you to separate yourself from others. Consequently, if you are around others whose actions promote or teach guilt, you readily adopt those beliefs. Later in life it becomes natural for you to feel guilty in situations that resemble what you were taught as a child. The beliefs you hold are from past programming that you didn't consciously choose in the first place. For this reason, you aren't using free will.

In childhood, the process of accepting feelings of guilt takes place in your unconscious. You learned what you should feel guilty about by the reinforced actions and teachings of authority figures and institutions, from teachers, peers, social norms, and religious upbringing. What you may think is right or wrong is probably based on your upbringing. Whatever beliefs you directly or indirectly accepted as a child are reinforced by similar circumstances in your present life.

Until now, you may have automatically accepted what you feel guilty about, but everything is a belief, and you have the power to believe anything you want. You do not have to hold on to any way of thinking just because you were raised that way or because someone else tells you it's the "right" way to be. Releasing guilt helps you become the master of your own life!

Harboring guilt keeps you from experiencing life and situations you may need as Soul. When you free yourself from the restraints of guilt, you open yourself up to new experiences you previously denied. As you let go of behavior created by guilt, other people may not understand or accept your life, your responses, or your reasons for needing certain experiences. You are the one who needs to validate your life and worth. Only you can give yourself the permission to live your life the way you need it to be. The more you accept guilt, the more you live from other people's points of view of how the world should be and what is right. Their beliefs may be perfect for them, but not for you. This is what you need to remember. By releasing guilt, you give yourself freedom to be your authentic self!

It takes courage to stand independent of the crowd. This is exactly what you do when you refuse to feel guilty. You release the limiting chains around your own life that interfere with your growth as Soul. The first step in being your own person is to do what your heart tells you to do. Releasing guilt from your heart is a phase of your independence. This makes more room for Divine Love.

Buying Into Guilt

So much of your life is probably lived on "automatic." You may have been trained to be polite and obliging when family members want your time or when friends or associates want you to do something. You may have a hard time asserting yourself. Saying "no" when you don't want to do something or when you don't have the time to do something for someone else is almost unknown. If you do something you really don't want to do because you feel guilty, you will end up feeling resentful and angry. You feel this way because you are going against what creates value for you. If you really want to do the things requested of you, that's another matter — then you are creating value because you are in total agreement with the request.

There are people in life who are on committees they don't want to be on and running errands they don't want to do, but they do them anyway out of guilt. Every time you do something out of guilt or harbor guilt in your life regarding some action you have taken, the more you are controlled by guilt and the less you are living the full, joyful life you could be living. Your life is now controlled by unconscious beliefs you absorbed as a child.

Many people trap themselves in the realm of how others think they should live. You can choose to live freely. You can live a life perfect for you and, in the process, grow incredibly instead of living a limited existence dictated by others' values or beliefs. You can achieve the life you want by releasing and refusing to accept guilt and all its trappings.

For example, I was raised to believe marriage was for life. My mother and father did not believe in divorce, and the Catholic Church taught that divorce was not part of God's plan. The seeds for guilt surrounding divorce were already planted in my unconscious mind when I married for the first time. I believed I should stay married for life, no matter what happened.

During the harder times in that marriage, I fleetingly thought of divorce, but I kept letting my guilt run my life. I believed I was responsible for Greg's happiness, and that I had to stay married to him forever, no matter what. These beliefs ruled my existence, and my growth as a person was stagnating. I was in therapy during this time, but even with therapy, I couldn't be honest with myself because I was too afraid I might leave my husband if I were to be really honest about what I needed as a person. Part of me was aware of what was transpiring, but I chose to ignore my need to leave my marriage. Guilt was the biggest reason I stayed with Greg as long as I did.

When I broke through the barriers of guilt, I realized it was best for me to divorce. Greg also came to that realization. If I had let guilt rule my life, I believe I would still be married to Greg, and my growth would have been stalled, or maybe never attained in this lifetime. Instead, I followed my inner voice of what was right for my life. I realized I was not responsible for anyone else's life, not even my husband's. No one can live another person's life or another person's values. I had to come to terms with my perceived responsibility regarding Greg.

Now I am not recommending that everyone who is unhappy in marriage chuck it and move on. What I am proposing is that you honestly look and see if your actions are out of guilt and the "shoulds" (as I call guilt), or if you are living as the true master of your destiny and director of your life. Answer this for yourself. It may take months or years of internal questioning. Give yourself time, and love yourself through any difficult decision or process you may confront.

Repressed Guilt

You also can harbor guilt in your body and not realize it. Guilt can manifest as sickness or other physical disorders. This may be harder to spot. If you find yourself sick, ask yourself if you are harboring guilt. Let yourself be honest, and the answers will come to you.

Guilt is energy, as is anger, and when guilt manifests in your body, it has been in your thinking for a while. Your body has the densest energy of all the parts that compose you as a person. When you have physical symptoms or sickness, your issue with your guilt is either very intense or of longstanding. Basically, guilt energy is trapped in the denser energy that makes up your body.

Let me give you a very powerful example of repressed guilt I encountered with a client. This client came to me to lose about twenty pounds. As I do with all my clients, I asked for a detailed personal history.

This woman's weight problem started five years earlier.

She had never before had a problem with weight. This was significant, and I wondered what might have occurred five years ago to trigger her weight gain.

As she recapped her life, she told me she had an abortion. I asked her during the session if she felt any guilt over the abortion. She said she didn't because she needed the abortion to save her life. I could tell she honestly didn't feel any conscious guilt. Therefore I proceeded in each session to encourage her to change her habits regarding food and exercise.

After several sessions, she still didn't lose weight, though she was eating right and exercising. She should have been losing weight if no emotional problem was involved. Once again I went back over her history and approached the subject of her abortion. This time I got more details, details that incorporated beliefs from her childhood. She told me she was raised in a fundamentalist religion. I asked her about the religion's belief regarding abortion, and you can guess what her answer was! The church strictly forbade abortion, and its teachings were laden with guilt and shame.

I felt she was hiding guilt from herself that showed up as self-punishment in the form of body fat because she had the abortion about the same time she started gaining weight. I told her I was going to give her some suggestions in hypnosis that would help her release her unconscious guilt. Her unconscious mind would work with her conscious desire to lose weight, and then she would reach her goal.

The next week she reported she had lost five and a half pounds! She hadn't changed her eating habits or the amount of exercise she was doing. She then realized how powerful thoughts and emotions were in her life and how she could punish herself without being conscious of guilt or beliefs.

To change the mental and emotional processes of guilt to

ones of love and positive self-acceptance, you have to understand that ALL guilt is self-punishment. It limits you from
receiving love from others, yourself, and Spirit. It is a negating
way to be, and it is most definitely not a way to help your self
grow. Guilt uses your emotional, mental, or physical energy to
stop you from being open and happy. Guilt negatively affects
the every level of your being.

All aspects of yourself and the forms of your energy can
change. If you can picture energy as either open and expansive
or closed and restrictive, then you get a clearer idea of what you
are doing when you allow guilt in your life. Guilt is restrictive in
nature. The qualities of this emotion are of limitation and clo-
sure. Love, on the other hand, is expansive and limitless.

How Guilt Feels

*To get a clearer understanding of the difference
in the quality and feeling of love as opposed to
guilt, take a quiet moment and feel and picture
your heart filled with love. Notice how it feels
in your body. You will probably find your heart
area feeling warm, open, or expansive, maybe even
lighter.*

*Now, immediately think of a situation that elicits
guilt for you and focus your attention on that.*

*I bet it takes no time at all to sense or feel the dif-
ference between the two energies. If I could guess, I
bet you felt heavier or darker with the guilt, maybe
even sick to your stomach. Most people, when they
take the time, can clearly distinguish between the
two states.* ⌒

This was just a short experiment. Imagine what guilt energy does to your body when you hold it for a longer time! The more you clear yourself of guilt and understand the true effects of guilt on your whole being, the happier and healthier you will be.

Guilt As Manipulation

The use of guilt is pervasive. People have used it for centuries to manipulate others to do what they want. Religions and governments have used it to keep people from being independent, keeping them from true growth. Guilt is abusive when used by anyone as a tool of manipulation. When you use guilt to manipulate others, you do it to have power and control over them.

An argument for guilt has been that if people didn't feel guilty, they would become savage and world chaos would result. I believe this would not happen because I feel people's basic nature is an inner drive to know themselves as Soul. This is a drive toward giving and receiving Divine Love. There will always be people who break laws — this is a given. Everyone is at a different state of development, and some Souls learn their lessons in terrible, hurtful ways, no matter what. But I believe the vast majority of the human race wants to grow and be happy. I feel if people like you and I release guilt more often, we can open ourselves to new experiences that are good for us. With our happiness and new expansive lives, we can help others grow.

Exercise

Release Guilt

The easiest way to release guilt is in the moment when you are aware of it. In that moment make a conscious decision to not buy into it. Either imagine giving it back to the other person or take a moment and breathe out guilt as a dark energy from your stomach area until you feel that area of your body become lighter. Then breathe in a color of light that represents to you love, worth, or joy. ᔐ

Fear

Fear is another emotion that restricts your life. It restricts your actions and happier emotions. It restricts your blood vessels and physically affects your body. Fear is not an emotion most people willingly confront or desire, but you may be experiencing more fear than you realize. Stress, which is such a common part of our lives, is really a mild form of fear. This may surprise many of you, but stress in your body is a physiological result of fear.

Mechanics of Fear

Fear is basic to being human, and it helps you survive. Instinctively, you respond to threats through the "fight or flight" syndrome. It is instinctual, and it was passed down to you from your primitive ancestors who continually experienced and responded to life-and-death situations. At times of perceived danger, the body releases more adrenalin into your bloodstream. The added adrenalin helps your body respond quickly and more effectively confront or avoid danger.

Primitive humans used their bodies to ward off attacks, and the physical activity balanced and used the added adrenalin. Today physical threats to your life are not as obvious and society encourages nonviolent behavior, though modern living affords many opportunities to feel threatened. Unlike those of our primitive ancestors, the threats are not always physical or the circumstances such that a person should fight back physically. This results in excess adrenalin because you are not physically using your body to ward off the attacks, and excess adrenalin can make you feel stressed out.

The "life-threatening" occurrences of your daily life are now things like coming up short on monthly bills, confronting rush hour traffic, or trying to escape the old thought patterns or negative ways of living. These seemingly non-threatening things cause much stress and unconscious fear.

Perceived Danger

It is not what happens to you that creates fear, but how you perceive and interpret situations with your thoughts and emotions. In modern life, most experiences with fear or stress come from perceived danger. Change or perceived danger creates stress, and stress keeps you from experiencing greater love, peace, and growth. You can eliminate a great deal of stress by effectively handling your beliefs, your thinking, and your emotional processes.

Karen, a former client in her mid-forties, is a graphic example of how changing perceptions can create a new life. When Karen first came to me, she said she felt unmotivated, uncaring about life, and tired of everything. She wanted to sleep all the time. She felt like she was putting on a mask for society, hiding her true feelings and herself. Karen said she saw everything as a threat, but she was open to new teaching and ready to change.

Well, right away, I started to reeducate her unconscious thinking process about guilt and anger from her childhood, giving her permission to feel long-repressed feelings safely and appropriately. At the same time, I taught her about higher Spiritual concepts and self-love. Fear of rejection and not being loved was at the core of her problem, so we did inner work on unconditional love and self-acceptance. Within two months, she felt like a different person.

At her last session Karen related how her life had been recently. She said she felt "cozy in her skin, warm and good, and no different than other people." She also said that she felt at peace with herself and that her fear of people was gone. She appreciated others as "beings of light" and did not get entangled in their negativity. Her husband noticed a change in her and loved her emerging new self. She commented, "Without fear you can love someone better and accept the love they have to share." Karen also said, "I feel the change that took six or seven weeks with you would have taken six or seven years someplace else."

Karen's comments are typical of the feedback I get all the time. The ones who are honest with themselves and ready to grow, like Karen, accept new teachings more deeply and more readily. The basic point here is that changing your perspective about life and what is real does affect every part of your life for the better.

A Different Perspective

Your perceptions about what is dangerous are largely created from cultural programming. You formed beliefs about what to be afraid of by the way you were raised. For example, people of primitive cultures have very different beliefs about what to fear than you do. Much of what you consider permanent and dangerous can be changed by changing your thoughts and by allowing yourself to view life from a different perspective, just like Karen!

I want to share a story my great friend Beth told me to illustrate this point in a different way. One Sunday we were at her house on the deck doing what we do best together — talking! It was one of those outstanding Indian Summer days; the leaves were perfect and the temperature was warm and balmy.

Beth has a cute little dog named Huey, and we were watching Huey play with his favorite toy, a little red ball. As we were throwing the ball to Huey and talking, Beth had a great flash of awareness about fear and how it restricts your life. Huey is a big chicken when it comes to walking up or down steps. He is a little dog, and steps pose a big problem for him. He doesn't like to go down the steps alone and when his ball rolled down the deck steps and into the backyard, Huey got frightened. We observed Huey trying to figure out how to get the ball without going downstairs. Huey kept looking at Beth, "asking" her to carry him or get the ball for him, but Beth stood firm. She wanted Huey to conquer his fear.

Beth said Huey's fear reminded her of people when they are afraid to change or try something new. People want this "new thing" in their lives but are afraid to leave old familiar surroundings to get it. They are paralyzed and may even try to have someone else take responsibility for them because they are afraid to do it themselves. What seems so frightening is really just little steps to a new awareness or to the prize you seek. What holds you back is not the situation, but the *perceived* danger involved in the new step to growth. **Most of what you fear is illusion!**

Beth finally gave Huey a helpful shove down the first step, and he managed the rest himself. Once Huey got down the steps he became engrossed in the back yard. Because this was a new experience for him, he started to sniff around and soon he lost interest in his ball. He found himself comfortable and happy in his new surroundings!

Beth observed if you just take the first step into a new way of thinking or action, before you know it you will find yourself fully participating in a new way of living. It soon feels fun and comfortable. When you overcome the barriers that keep you from your life's little red ball, you find your fear about the new experience was an illusion!

Taking Action

Fear and guilt can hinder love and experiences of growth, and guilt and fear can create barriers to deeper relationships. Fear prevents you from opening your heart with love for others because you don't feel safe to be yourself. Guilt limits the way you live your life, restricting what you experience. If you want to rid yourself of fear and guilt, you must be sincere in your desire and consistently act to change your old patterns and beliefs regarding fear and guilt.

You can sit around all day long and think you want to change, but if you don't take action you stay in the victim role. **Actions speak louder than words!** You need to want to change with the same intensity and commitment as a person who is dying of thirst wants water. That person is not only thinking of water but will do anything to get it. To change your life and evolve into higher states of awareness you must have that kind of desire, and back it up with committed actions. It is up to you to find what you need; then you will not be dependent on anyone telling you how to live. Your inner, true self (Soul) will direct you to the right vehicle or method, which will be perfect for your growth at that time. The growth or change you seek is an ongoing process, but even a journey of a thousand miles begins with the first step. If you don't take that step, you will never reach your destination.

Please feel free to try the exercises that follow. If you find that nothing here helps you, experiment with other tools and ways to grow. The stronger your desire is to change, the faster you will find tools to accomplish your change. As your consciousness and your spiritual vision expand, tools you used before may take on new meaning. Be assured you can release old thought patterns that no longer serve you. It takes your actions combined with sincerity to do this.

All these exercises can be used to release guilt or fear. Use them when you want to either change or release emotion. As with any of the exercises in this book, keep in mind you may have to do them for a while. They can be even more powerful in combination with other techniques, courses, or therapy. No one tool is effective for all cases.

Without consistent actions, no change will occur. Be open in your life to all vehicles that will help you grow.

Releasing Fear and Guilt

1. The opposite of fear is feeling safe. Ask yourself if "feeling safe" were a color of light, what color would it be? Let yourself know. This is an intuitive process. When you sense a color check its energy by visualizing the color going through your body. If you feel calmer in any sense or more peaceful, you picked the right color. Color is a vibration that feeds you on an unconscious, spiritual level. Most of my clients pick blue, but you can use any color, except black. Take at least five minutes and close your eyes and breathe in the color of your choice. Breathe out the fear as black. Do this very slowly, breathing from your abdomen, and not your chest.

2. Get comfortable. Chant a high vibratory word for about five minutes. Close your eyes and see your guilt or fear as a picture. Shrink the picture, making it smaller and smaller, until it fits in the palm of your hand. If the picture was dark in color change it to light. Now break up the picture into tiny, little pieces. One at a time, throw each piece away or put it far behind you until you can no longer see it.

3. Use affirmations regarding your fear or guilt. Start each affirmation with, "I am safe." Some of these can look like this.

I am safe to feel comfortable while flying.

I am safe to release my guilt about _____.

I am feeling safer and safer everyday.

Make up your own affirmations and put them in the present tense. Write them each day.

4. Get comfortable and chant a high vibratory word, like HU, for a few minutes. Visualize yourself above your body and time. Look down on your

Exercise

> *situation and ask Spirit to help you see it from a higher perspective. If the situation looks dark, change it to a bright color and see yourself handling it without guilt or fear. Then look to the future and see it getting brighter and brighter because you handled the situation in a healthier way — without fear or guilt.*

Keep working at releasing guilt or fear when they come up in your life. The more positive actions you take to change your old limiting patterns, the faster you become the master of your life. Create new empowering patterns of thinking and acting. Don't let your old ways of thinking and living master you!

CHAPTER TEN

Values of the Higher Self

When we live our lives
from rules and wants
of the little self…
the results of such
ensnare our light within.

As we evolve,
And live from the light
of what can be…
this day
becomes elevated for all to see.

Kindness and love to share.
These are the new rules to live by:
Our new life, our new awareness,
abundant with the warmth of love
and light
endlessly, timelessly, now!

This chapter discusses ways of living and thinking for your greater spiritual advancement. These values, the higher aspects of living, affect all dimensions of your life. These higher values help you get in contact with yourself as Soul. I invite you to experiment and learn how they affect your quality of life and inner connection with Spirit and God.

In each moment you choose how to live, and the choices you make affect your life. With each action you take you are telling life who you are and where you are going. The causes you make with your actions create who you are in each moment. Whether the actions you make in your life are judgments, thinking patterns, or physical actions, they are consistently creating who you are. Consequently, your actions either raise or lower your vibrations or consciousness; you either open yourself to Spirit or move away from connecting with Spirit.

I am not telling you to live any certain way. I definitely believe each person grows in the way that is best for him or her. This chapter is intended to help uplift your awareness and speed your spiritual growth no matter what path you have choose. Consistency of your total actions, **not just intellectual understanding**, is key to your growth in the spiritual realms as well as in the physical ones.

No awareness or change is achieved overnight. The more you allow yourself to change with Divine Love and acceptance, the deeper and more real the change will be.

Detachment

Many spiritual leaders talk about detachment as an important perspective to acquire for your highest growth, but the idea of detachment is very misunderstood. Detachment, simply stated, is living from a state of awareness in which whatever happens in your life is okay. By "okay," I mean you realize whatever happens to you creates the perfect circumstances for your growth as Soul. When you live from this detached state you let go of internal attachments associated with your ego and emotional struggles about how things in your life "ought" to be. All the "shoulds," "oughts," and "have-to-be-this-ways" fall away from your ego and thinking. Detachment is a state of awareness where Spirit guides your life, instead of your ego telling you what to do. It is working with your highest powers instead of your small, limited human ego. With detachment you live with the awareness that all things change. When you don't get what your ego wants, or circumstances are different than what you expect, you find it is no big deal.

With a detached attitude you can enjoy life more completely, because your consciousness is more fully in the now. You are less concerned with what is or isn't in your life at the present moment. Living from a more objective viewpoint, you become less attached to daily life around you. When you are not as immersed in the things or the circumstances, you don't suffer when things don't go as you planned. Detachment is a state of mind and Spirit. You realize all the things in your life except Soul and Spirit are not permanent. You enjoy what there is to enjoy and feel what there is to feel, but you are grounded to the core of your true self as Soul. You "go with the flow" of life, without becoming swept away over change in your present circumstance.

Detachment — Focus on Spirit

With detachment, you are aware everything on Earth will pass on, change, or die. Detachment keeps you focused on the true purpose of life, Soul's growing toward God. Your daily life is a drama to teach Soul what it needs. The less you are attached

to material outcomes, the more you can grow in spiritual awareness. Detachment makes Soul the controlling aspect of your life,
not your ego. Detachment can be difficult to attain because
your ego constantly tries to control you. Your will constantly
tries to get its own way.

If you understand that Spirit forms everything you know
of as life, you know Spirit is more powerful than your ego. Spirit
always exists. Your ego and will are from the physical realm, and
their nature is limited.

What you likely do every day is put your ego and will
above Spirit, but when you live life this way you become very
attached to outcomes. You want things to go the way your ego
or your emotions want them to go, or you focus on the comforts
of the physical body. When you live strictly from ego you suffer
more and your actions are not for your highest ultimate good.

Attachment Leads to Pain

Attachment to things and circumstances leads to pain
because all life is change. Pain comes because you want tran-
sitory things to always be in your life. Unconsciously or consciously, you think they will fulfill you.

This doesn't mean you can't feel deeply for people or
enjoy life, or that you can't have goals. Your greatest lessons are
to be had in the present. To deny your present reality is
escapism. I believe detachment is a marriage of the material
world and the spiritual. Your actions should be directed from
your highest self, not one that is limited. When you do this,
detachment is achieved, and at the same time, you can live a full
physical life.

Part of living a full physical life encompasses making goals.
The detached way of making goals is to ask Spirit to bring whatever is best for your deepest good and the deepest good of others. Let go of any strong energy or attachment to what you
want. You will always get what is best for your highest growth

when you create goals in this manner. Very simply put, Spirit is always on your side.

When you live from the consciousness of detachment, you let Spirit guide you. It is being of the world yet not part of it. Live fully and enjoy what there is to enjoy. Know the drama of this life is not the real you, it is but a dream. **The real you is Soul!**

Attachment Affects Outcome

A good example of how attachment to an outcome can negatively affect your life is what happened when I met my first husband, Greg. At that time, I was just becoming aware of personal power in my life, and I was mostly using my personal power from the attached state of my ego. I used positive thinking to try to control situations, people, and circumstances. I thought the best thing for us was to get married, and I used my will and energy to make it happen. Well, Greg did ask me to marry him even though he still had many doubts about marriage. (His strong doubts were not about his love for me but whether it was right for him as an individual to get married at that time.)

Because of my attachment to being married and the intense energy I placed on this situation, I feel I influenced him to go through with the marriage. I do realize I am not responsible for his decision, but all things are energy, and energy affects life. I was very attached to the outcome of his decision, and I did not give it to Spirit and ask for my higher good. Since I was coming from what my ego wanted, I feel my attachment affected his decision. We eventually got married, but we weren't happy.

Greg was unhappy because he had unfinished business regarding his own growth, and his unhappiness affected me. If I had let Spirit guide me, I believe the hard lessons I learned through the marriage might have been lessened.

Detachment Leads to Growth

Now I try to use my ego and will in conjunction with Spirit. I realize I truly am Soul and I want to be the most conscious, most highly evolved person I can be. Spirit, the forming energy of life, is here for my good and I am learning to trust its guidance.

One way to help yourself let go of attachment and the pull of your ego is to do some form of spiritual exercise each day. Ask for guidance from God or Spirit to learn and be shown whatever you need for your spiritual growth. When you start each day this way, you discover that working with Spirit is a lot easier than with your pure will. You will be led to answers and develop in ways your will or ego cannot possibly imagine. When you work with Spirit you work with the forming stuff of all of life, and your attachments of how things have to be drop away.

As I allow and trust Spirit to use me as a channel, my life has opened up incredibly — spiritually, personally, emotionally, and financially. The basic, fundamental aspect of Spirit is abundance and joy. The more you come from dedicating your actions as a vehicle or channel for Spirit, the more you are guided to your highest good. The less you are attached to results your ego wants and the more you realize that whatever is happening to you is perfect for your growth and happiness, the more peaceful and happy you become. Trust and peace start to develop when you live your life from detachment. Detachment does not mean you are passive or a victim. Detachment is actually an active state where you know and feel your partnership with God and Spirit.

Non-interference

Another aspect of detachment is letting go of controlling others, or non-interference. Many times, whether you are aware of it or not, you live your life trying to control other people. You may do this in direct or subtle ways.

Trying to change others and force your beliefs or your way of living on them is interference. It's getting into other people's space and trying to direct them, such as telling them how they must feel or manipulating them through guilt. When you do this, you interfere with their rights as Soul to be, as they need to be, even if they are choosing to consciously or unconsciously be a victim. All of us have the right to live the way we need to as long as we don't interfere with anyone else's rights.

This doesn't mean you can never make suggestions to help people. Interference comes into play when you have an **attachment** to the outcome of your suggestion, or when you force your will or energy into their space. Sit back and think about this. How many times have you given suggestions when your energy or intent was attached to having a situation go your way? How many times have you been intent on someone doing something they didn't want to do because you absolutely *knew* they had to "for their own good?" This is attachment.

This lesson can be hard to learn. Many times you care so much that you interfere with others' lives. Your ego thinks it knows what is best for this person's growth, but you are interfering when you force your energy on someone to change. Your ego is attached to the results and thinks its way is the only way. The most blatant form of interference is physical abuse; subtler forms of interference involve the use of your energy from your emotional self or mind. As you become more aware and conscious, you will discern subtler examples of interference. As you become less attached to how other people should live, your life blossoms.

One benefit of becoming more awakened to how life works is discovering that you can consciously take actions to create more harmony, balance, love, and joy. Letting go of interfering in other people's lives is a giant step towards creating harmony in your life!

Interference happens many times when you think you are

actually helping. When you take responsibility away from others, you help them stay victims. This is what happens in unhealthy relationships. Remember, it's not that you can't give suggestions to others; **it's your attachment to the other person doing what you suggested that causes interference.** Put very simply, you are trying to control another Soul. This can be very hard at times to keep in perspective. By letting go of interfering with someone's thoughts and life, you create positive changes in your life.

For example, I would be interfering as a life coach if I were attached to the outcome and potential growth of my clients — that would be abusing my power as their coach. I would be interfering and controlling if I forced a client to stay in sessions longer than he or she wanted to. The force could be no more than a strong suggestion that had my energy attached to it but I would be taking responsibility away from them. Interference can be badgering your mate to quit smoking, or constantly telling someone how to do something because you think it is the only right way.

The more your consciousness grows, the more you become aware of personal boundaries and how your energy or actions may be interfering with others. Allow yourself to discover ways you stop your growth through interference.

For example, how often have you had an opinion and thought another person wrong or stupid just because he or she didn't agree with you? How often have you tried to change someone's mind to what *you* considered was right? This is interference. Only you know if you are consciously interfering with another's personal space or boundaries, their thoughts or personal beliefs. When you feel someone is interfering with you, it is your right to stand up for yourself and protect your personal boundaries.

Interference Through Prayer

You are even interfering when you pray to change someone in any way if you do not have the person's permission to do so. This is true even if they are sick. If you have permission to pray for someone, structure your prayer and energy regarding the person's welfare so you let God and Spirit do what is for their highest good. Be careful not to be attached to the outcome.

There are many situations where you may want to help another person or to pray for them. I think it is extremely hard to not do something for someone who is living like a victim, or not to pray for recovery when a person is sick.

When my father was dying of cancer, I had to stop myself from praying for his recovery. I gave my desire and will to Spirit and I asked for his highest good to manifest. The recovery of my father may not have been for his highest good as Soul.

This may sound strange but some people actually need difficult experiences to help them. Individuals *must* learn their own lessons regarding their life to progress to the next step in spiritual development. If you take those experiences away from them, they may still need the lessons at some time in their development as Soul. The most expedient way to help people is to let them grow in their own way and in their own time. Neither you nor anyone else is graced with supreme wisdom to know what is best for another. This is why it is always best to give it to God.

Trusting and Surrender

Trusting Spirit to guide your life is a fundamental lesson each Soul has to learn. Another name for trust with regards to Spirit is surrender. It is not an easy thing to explain or an easy concept to grasp.

Trust sounds simple, but it evokes so many emotions from previous concepts that trusting is not easy to do or describe. Let me try.

Until recently, it had been hard to allow others and (more importantly) Spirit into my life, to help and guide me. I was on my own at an early age. But even when I lived at home, I always felt I had no one but myself to rely on. Because of that, I felt vulnerable if I asked for help or trusted someone else to help me. Consequently, I have had a hard time trusting or surrendering my will and the direction of my life to Spirit.

Another reason I had a hard time with surrendering is because I encountered people who relinquished responsibility for their lives and lived as victims, thinking God would do their work for them. I am emphatically against this! I have grown because I accept responsibility for my life, and I am not about to give up and be a victim. Being responsible means doing all you can do both in your outer life and helping yourself grow inwardly. This higher aspect of responsibility has given me a feeling of control and power over my life I never experienced before!

Therefore how do you take responsibility for your life and surrender and trust Spirit at the same time? Remember cause and effect: The more actions you make to connect with Spirit and let Spirit guide your life the more you will find Spirit guiding your life. This happens in conjunction with the responsibility you take in your life. This is the marked difference. You can't effectively live your life if you live it as a child waiting for God to change your life without action from yourself. Surrender is a marriage of self-responsibility and uniting with Spirit. You have to make all the actions you possibly can and, at the same time, ask for guidance of the highest order from God and the Holy Spirit. Surrender is a balancing of strong self-responsibility and hearing and accepting Spirit's guidance in your life.

The more your actions are based on trust, the more trust you will develop. Some individuals have more to learn about the responsibility side of this process, while others have to ease into the trusting, guiding part. Know like everything else in life, it is a process. Trust is formed step by step. It does not happen overnight. Because of all my years relying on myself and being responsible, it felt strange at first to let the Holy Spirit into my life, to trust what was happening was for my growth and higher development. But the more I surrender my will and ego to Spirit while taking responsible actions for my growth, the happier my life becomes and the more I feel the presence of God in my life.

In surrendering, I am not negating my responsibilities of growth to someone else or even to God. I am working in partnership with the higher aspect of all life, which is Spirit. I am learning the Holy Spirit promotes my good and abundance through my mind, body, emotions, and Soul. Even if I experience something I'd prefer I didn't, I am learning it is the easiest and fastest route to my happiness. When I used my will alone, situations would manifest in my life that were far from easy and good, and my life was much more of a struggle.

Partnership with Spirit

How do you know when you are in partnership with Spirit? It is like trying to describe what falling in love feels like — you know it when you experience it. The two are very similar. You will know when you are in partnership with Spirit. It is beyond logic and reason.

When I come from my ego I feel more stress and I do not feel as loving or tuned into life. When I come from my heart during my contemplations and dedicate my actions as a vehicle to the Holy Spirit, my whole day has a different feeling. I feel more relaxed about everything and more protected. I have more inner peace. I still do all the things I want and need to do to live on this planet, but because of this partnership and dedication to Spirit, the actions I take from work to play and everything in between, become filled with purpose. My life is no longer a series of empty actions to fill up time. The whole of my life is transformed into something profound. From the time you dedicate your actions and self to Spirit, nothing in your life is inconsequential. Your whole life becomes filled with purpose. You will know you are working with the Holy Spirit.

In the process of surrendering my life to Spirit, I make responsible decisions but I feel less alone. Before, it felt like me against the world. Now I feel the world and I are partners. I feel I am always protected. It's similar to studying a martial art with a wonderful master teacher. With the teacher you learn more quickly and effectively with less damage to your body, because the master is guiding you. Without the master you could still learn, but it could take longer and your injuries might be more severe. We all have the freedom to choose. You can go your whole life alone or you can choose to have help. As with the master martial arts instructor, the teacher does not do the work for you. He or she is there to guide you and make your progress faster and easier.

Faith

Another important value to help you live life more deeply is faith. One aspect of faith is realizing something is true. It is formed by the proof of your experience, not because someone has told you it is true. Faith is also a process, as are trust and surrender. Faith can start as an inkling that a concept might be true. Then, with testing and experience, your faith can grow.

Faith is not something that can be pushed on you. It is developed through your inner knowing. No matter what someone teaches, don't have faith in it until it rings true for you. If you have faith in something just because an authority tells you to believe, you take responsibility away from yourself. True faith is knowing in your heart that something is true for you, and it is the freedom to decide to hold on to or let go of what is true for you. Faith is an evolution. No matter what, faith is not a passive state. Living your life with faith is dynamic and action-oriented!

Let it unfold for you!

Having faith is different from relinquishing responsibility and power within yourself — you need to always discern if a teaching is right for you. Most people equate faith to giving up personal power, but having faith is empowering because it is an inner knowing no one can take away from you. Develop faith because of your own understandings, not because a minister, teacher, or someone else has told you what to believe.

Similarly, if someone constantly treats you with respect and love, your knowledge and experience of your friendship and faith in that person is real. No matter what anyone tells you, you have your own experience. No one can convince you otherwise. Your faith in your friendship was developed by actions taken by both of you. You did not develop faith because you were told to believe in someone. You have faith in that relationship because of your *experience* of it.

Faith As An Inner Awareness

Faith can also start as an inner awareness that something can be done or achieved. This awareness can be nurtured by your actions and the proof you encounter. It's similar to wanting to learn something new. First, you have the idea that you can learn or do a particular thing. As you continue with this new endeavor, your faith in yourself and your skill grows. With faith you can achieve tremendous things in your life.

A great way to increase your faith is to cultivate the attitude of be, do, and then have. The most powerful way to create things and change in your life is to first *be* the person inwardly you need to be. Then make all the actions needed (*do*), and you will achieve the proper results (*have*). The more conviction you have, the faster your life changes.

For example, suppose you want more money in your life. You have to first examine your beliefs. In my own life I wanted money and financial independence because I felt they would give me more security. As I continued to grow in awareness, I realized I have to first achieve that security within myself before changes can occur in my outer environment. Nothing on the outside of your life can change until you first change your inner self. When you do, the energy shift will change your outer environment.

Because what I truly desired was security, I have been concentrating on making my inner self feel more secure and safe, with or without money. This point is important! You need to be the way you want to be in your inner self first (even if you don't have what you want on the outside of your life), before these results manifest physically.

The formula for making more money might be like this: First feel with the inner core of yourself that you already have the things you want. Next, take appropriate outer actions to change your financial picture. Set goals, visualize results, do all the outer actions you need to do to receive money. Then release your desire with faith to Spirit. Every time I follow this formula for change, I create what I want in the most efficient way I can imagine. At the same time, I am growing from my highest self because I have released attachments to specific outcomes. The more I let Spirit guide me, the happier I become.

Appreciation

Part of "be" encompasses appreciating what's in your life right now. Appreciation is an attitude of abundance, whether or not you have the thing(s) in your life you want. The more you express appreciation and feel it in your heart, the more abundance will be manifested for you in your life.

The state of appreciation is so powerful I can't emphasize it enough! The more you focus on appreciating your life now, the more you set up causes that emphasize abundance. Feeling thankful is an action of acknowledgement for what is in your life right now. Often people complain about what they don't have and emphasize it with their thoughts or words. When they do this, they focus on lack instead of abundance. Remember, what you focus on you attract. When you focus on appreciation you focus on abundance instead of lack. With appreciation you set your life in motion to receive even more! You create actions that manifest abundance.

When your heart is filled with appreciation you open your heart up for more Divine Love and Spirit. You relax, and in your relaxed state you contact Spirit. When you are tense you tend to shut down your flow with Spirit, which shuts down your power to create and receive.

A great way to develop more appreciation is to write down each day between five and ten things for which you are grateful. These things can be as simple as being grateful that you can see, have friends, had food today, etc. The power is in the act of writing and acknowledging your appreciation for what is in your life right now!

Blessing a Situation

Another attitude to help you see things from a broader perspective comes from blessing any situation that is hard to handle. Say to yourself, "I bless this situation in the name of God," or "May the blessings be." You are not trying to control any feelings or people — you are raising your vibrations. With this action you release control over any particular outcome, asking to be led to a higher way of interacting. This helps you to be free of the pull of any lower energy attachment that your mind or ego might create or any negative energy from someone else.

Suppose, for instance, there is someone you see frequently whose physical appearance or personality turns you off. It might be easy to put down or feel disgusted with the person. Neither action raises your consciousness. To keep yourself from lowering your vibrations and putting negative energy toward another, say to yourself, "May the blessings be," or "In the name of God." You are not trying to change the other person. You are blessing the situation to raise your thought processes and vibrations so you can be above any negative mental or emotional causes. Whenever you are linked with the Holy Spirit, fear and pettiness leave you and, once again Divine Love flows through your life.

In my own life, I find myself silently blessing a situation when I need to get above my negativity or worry. It helps calm me down and raises my consciousness in the process. It helps my human mind remember why I am here.

The whole point of this book is to help you realize spiritual principles are not separate from your life. Lovingly use these guides. The more you integrate Spirit into your life, the more your physical life manifests this change. A spiritual integration of life is not an intellectual understanding or an esthetic practice. Spiritual integration is a vibrant, whole life. Every level of your existence, from Soul to your physical body, is positively affected by your using these laws and the Divine Love of Spirit.

Conclusion

Spirituality is not just for when you die, it is for your life right now! *There is only NOW!* Wherever you go, even in death, there is only now. Wherever you find yourself, use the moment you have to grow to your fullest. Spiritual growth is never separate from where you are in the moment. If you separate your spiritual life from your daily life or wait until you die to understand life, you are missing your chance for growth.

Live life with all the zest and joy you can muster. Have the multitudes of experiences you desire. *You are Soul.* Soul is here to learn. You learn from doing. Be, do, and have! Let Spirit guide your learning. Boundless joy and love are waiting for you when you live from this higher awareness!

May the blessings be!

About the Author

Marian Massie is a Hypnotherapist/Success Coach and founder and president of Advanced Perceptions, Inc. Since 1985, Marian has helped thousands of people reach their personal, financial and career goals through her individual sessions and seminars. She gets results because she blends her unique application of hypnotherapy/coaching coupled with methods drawn from her own successful personal healing which she chronicles in this book.

Dear Readers,

I do want to hear from you! **Please do not send attachments with your emails,** I will NOT open any attachments! I am still seeing private clients, doing keynote talks, seminars and book signings. You or your organization can book an engagement or order products by calling 770-956-0554 or through my website, www.marianmassie.com